RACEN

REMARKABLE WOMEN OF THE TWENTIETH CENTURY

REMARKABLE WOMEN OF THE TWENTIETH CENTURY

100 PORTRAITS of ACHIEVEMENT

KRISTEN GOLDEN AND BARBARA FINDLEN

FOREWORD BY SHELLY LAZARUS
PREFACE BY FAITH POPCORN WITH ADAM HANFT

FRIEDMAN/FAIRFAX
PUBLISHERS

in association with

CORBIS

A FRIEDMAN/FAIRFAX BOOK

© 1998 by Michael Friedman Publishing Group, Inc.

Library of Congress Cataloging-in-Publication data

Golden, Kristen.

Remarkable women of the twentieth century / by Kristen Golden
and Barbara Findlen.

    p.   cm.

Includes bibliographical references and index.

ISBN 1-56799-599-3

1. Women—Biography.   2. Biography—20th century.   I. Findlen,
Barbara.   II. Title.

CT3235.G65 1998

920.72'09'04—dc21   98-22253

                                                    CIP

Editorial Director: Sharyn Rosart
Editor: Celeste Sollod
Art Director: Jeff Batzli
Designer: Milagros Sensat
Photography Editor: Amy Talluto
Production Manager: Camille Lee

Color separations by Radstock Repro
Printed in England by Butler & Tanner Limited

1 3 5 7 9 10 8 6 4 2

For bulk purchases and special sales, please contact:
Friedman/Fairfax Publishers
Attention: Sales Department
15 West 26th Street
New York, NY 10010
212/685-6610 FAX 212/685-1307

Visit our websites:
http://www.metrobooks.com
http://www.corbis.com

Dedication

To our daughter, Grace, a remarkable woman of the twenty-first century

Acknowledgments

First, we would like to thank our editor, Celeste Sollod, for giving us the opportunity to write this book, and giving us the editorial freedom to do it our own way. We appreciate her intelligent input and gentle guidance.

Rosella and Fred Findlen truly made the writing of this book possible by taking us in for days at a time—sharing their home and office with us, and showering their boundless energy and love on our daughter, Grace.

Our deepest gratitude to our friends who kept us fed and watered, especially Robert Strickstein; and Grace endlessly entertained, especially Sharon Lennon; and Anastasia Higginbotham, who somehow divined each time we were secretly flagging and sent us inspired encouragement.

Thanks to Kate Findlen for her tremendous generosity in providing us with the equipment and technical expertise we needed to write this book.

Rosalie Maggio's New Beacon Book of Quotations by Women was so fascinating that reading it threatened to derail the project. We thank her for her indispensible resource.

We appreciate the careful copyediting of Diane Boccadoro, whose sharp eyes and intelligent questions enhanced the manuscript. We were fortunate to work with a terrific photo editor, Amy Talluto, whose talent, ingenuity, and patience brought the stories in this book to life visually.

For their thoughtful brainstorming and meticulous research, we thank Betty and Sam Carter, Gayle Kirshenbaum, Amelia Richards, Jenny Pritchett, Dylan Siegler, B.J. Wishinsky, and the relentless Patsy McCarthy. We would also like to thank the personal assistants of many of the esteemed women profiled here, who took the time to help us create the best possible accounts of these women's lives. The National Women's History Project in Windsor, California, and the Upper Midwest Women's History Center in St. Paul, Minnesota, were instrumental in piecing together the herstories of the lesser-known women.

And our heartfelt thanks to Gloria Steinem, whose wisdom and personal knowledge informed our writing, and whose generosity and friendship continue to inspire us.

Contents

istory is filled with remarkable women—it is our good fortune to be living in a time when their accomplishments are recognized and rewarded. *Remarkable Women of the Twentieth Century* is a book about just some of these achievers.

"Remarkable" is an organizing principle called for in a century that has seen unprecedented achievement by women. Over the course of the last one hundred years, the contributions made by women have become more and more visible, with the result that women's place in society has been forever changed.

"Remarkable" is a category that is encompassing enough to allow us to celebrate the greatness of women without regard to some absolute, fixed notion of achievement. These women are remarkable for something greater. They matter.

When I am asked to talk about business success to women's groups, and especially to college students, this is what I tell them: You will do remarkable things if you are true to your spirit. This book is a testament to that potential.

The only thing this book does not chronicle is the legion of equally remarkable women who, but for the chance of time and history, are not celebrated—except, of course, in their own less public lives. No doubt every reader will know of someone who could have been included. Who will be included in the next century's edition? The first woman to become President of the United States, the first woman on Mars, the woman who cures cancer, the first female chairperson of IBM.... I anticipate with great pleasure seeing our daughters—and our daughters' daughters—fill those pages.

Shelly Lazarus

Shelly Lazarus
Chairman and CEO, Ogilvy & Mather

Preface

he book you hold in your hands is a living legacy that simultaneously inspires celebration and reflection. It inspires celebration because the astonishing range of accomplishment, depth of courage, and amplitude of talent that it documents are more than enough to summon forth our collective awe. It inspires reflection because it is impossible to read this book without wondering about all those women who would have, could have, made it to these pages were it not for the oppressive social structures in which they struggled.

Although this work is subtitled "100 Portraits of Achievement," the most compelling portrait of all is the big picture that is painted by the book in its entirety. It is one enormous, extraordinary canvas that depicts the very heart and soul of life in this century. We are who we are and what we are because of the contributions—often under the most punishing and unyielding of circumstances—of women.

In the last ten or twenty years, our public school textbooks have finally started to give women their historical due, celebrating their accomplishments in the shaping of our world in every area, every discipline, every vector. Hallelujah! To those who resist this much needed realignment of our history to include not just women, but people of color as well, I say: Buy this book, read this book, and then tell me that the textbooks of the past didn't ignore women, didn't bypass and marginalize some of the most important figures of the twentieth century.

Having said that, it is impossible not to be optimistic after reading this book. If women were able to accomplish this much in a society that held them back, working in institutions that restrained them, battling within families that often dismissed their dreams, then I am dazzled by the prospects for girls born today in our still imperfect, but vastly improved, world.

Some of the women in this book I have had the privilege of knowing. Others I have read about, studied, and admired. Yet there are some, I must confess, who I had not heard of, whose stories were new to me, and I suspect, will be new to you. This reinforces the importance of what Kristen Golden and Barbara Findlen have done; while a book acknowledging one hundred remarkable men of the twentieth century would no doubt be a retrospective of those icons we have already analyzed and fully documented, it is telling that a comparable paean to one hundred remarkable women contains so many fresh faces, untold stories, unilluminated triumphs.

While virtually any one of these women could serve as a controlling metaphor for this splendid book, from Eleanor Roosevelt to Carry Nation, from Rosa Parks to Marie Curie to Virginia Woolf, the woman I choose to represent the book as a whole is Virginia Apgar. I had not known, until I read this book, that she was the person behind the Apgar score. Virginia Apgar was one of the first women to graduate from Columbia University's College of Physicians and Surgeons. At the time, women could not become surgeons, so she entered what was still an embryonic field: anesthesiology.

The Apgar score, which she introduced in 1952, is well known to every nervous parent, grandparent, and godparent of a newborn. After attending more than 15,000 births, Apgar developed five criteria that measure the vigor and responsiveness of an infant. Every one of us born since then, man and woman, hero and knave, success and flop, has an Apgar score. The test that first established our individual capacity to change the world was developed by a woman. What can be more of an augury of women's potential than that?

In many ways, America is far ahead of much of the world in the opportunities it holds out to women. With that in mind, I'd like to use the forum of this preface to ask George Soros—who is by far the most creative and innovative philanthropist of our time—to buy one million copies of this book and distribute it to schools and other institutions all over the world, so the universal community of girls can be allowed to believe in their own, individual futures.

Best Future,

Faith

Faith Popcorn
Futurist and Bestselling Author

Introduction

I n the major events of the twentieth century, as well as in everyday life, the contributions of women are profound—and too often unsung. This book highlights just one hundred of the most remarkable, fascinating, and influential women of the century—leaders, creators, rebels, pioneers, stars, advocates, visionaries, revolutionaries, athletes, and daredevils whose achievements create a composite of this extraordinary era.

This collection is not exhaustive, nor is it meant to be exclusive. The diversity of women who have had significant impact on the twentieth century is truly amazing and can only be hinted at in glimpses of one hundred lives. Women have been key players in the important events and developments of the century: the world wars, women's suffrage, the Depression, the rise of mass media, the civil rights movement, feminism, and other revolutions. You will find women who are beloved and admired along with those who are controversial, as well as women of extraordinary accomplishment who are not household names.

Their lives reflect a fraction of the breadth of experience and contributions of women. All of these women could have volumes written about them, and many have. In their collected profiles you will find continuity (Mary Pickford, Lucille Ball, and Oprah Winfrey—the first, second, and third women to own Hollywood studios); extremes of opinion (anarchist Emma Goldman and conservative Margaret Thatcher); striking contradictions (Israeli Prime Minister Golda Meir and Palestinian leader Hanan Ashrawi); historical connections (Planned Parenthood founder Margaret Sanger and later Planned Parenthood president Faye Wattleton); varieties of styles (Rosa Parks, Carry Nation, Marilyn Monroe); and interesting juxtapositions (Nguyen Thi Binh, who negotiated the end of the Vietnam War, and Maya Lin, who designed the Vietnam Veterans Memorial).

We have organized the chapters thematically, and within each chapter the biographies are arranged chronologically by the period of each woman's strongest influence or most notable achievement. This structure offers a sense of the progress (or lack thereof) for women in this century, and also points to ways in which some women influenced or opened doors for those who came later.

We hope that this book will provoke thought about women's contributions to the twentieth century, discussion about women's roles and possibilities, and, of course, debate about who else could have been included.

—Kristen Golden and Barbara Findlen

Throughout the twentieth century, women whose deeds came from the heart made an indelible mark on the world around them. **Above:** Humanitarian Eleanor Roosevelt with Mary Pickford, the first female Hollywood mogul. **Right:** Grammy award-winning poet and performer Maya Angelou. **Below:** Amelia Earhart waves to the crowds who lined Broadway to welcome her home from her historic flight to Europe in 1932.

Chapter 1

AMAZING GRACE

Helen Keller, writer and lecturer

Gabrielle "Coco" Chanel, fashion designer

Georgia O'Keeffe, artist

Marian Anderson, singer

Wilma Rudolph, athlete

Barbra Streisand, singer, actor, director, and producer

Joni Mitchell, singer and songwriter

Martina Navratilova, athlete

Alice Walker, writer and poet

Maya Lin, architect

Meryl Streep, actor

⸺⟨⟩⸺

Dignity, style, and creativity—rare qualities, and rarer still when they are woven together in one person. The talents and accomplishments of these women leave us in awe.

Meryl Streep

Marian Anderson

Coco Chanel

Helen Keller

Georgia O'Keeffe

Barbra Streisand

Joni Mitchell

Alice Walker

Wilma Rudolph

Helen Keller
writer and lecturer (1880–1968)

I n *The Story of My Life*, Helen Keller relives the extraordinary moment when she—a deaf, blind, and mute six-year-old—first understood that words are symbols that have meaning. As her gifted teacher, Annie Sullivan, holds one of Keller's hands under a spout of water and rapidly spells the word "water" into her other hand, Keller recalled, "I stood still, my whole attention fixed upon the motions of her fingers. Suddenly I felt a misty consciousness as of something forgotten—a thrill of returning thought; and somehow the mystery of language was revealed to me.

I knew then that 'w-a-t-e-r' meant the wonderful cool something that was flowing over my hand." With Sullivan at her side for almost fifty years, Keller—a suffragist, feminist, pacifist, and socialist—became a prolific writer and impassioned lecturer, advocating for the rights of people with disabilities.

Born in Tuscumbia, Alabama, Keller lost her sight and hearing from a childhood illness (possibly scarlet fever) at the age of nineteen months. Locked in her own world, unable to communicate with her family, the bright child grew increasingly frustrated and wildly destructive. Her desperate parents brought her to Alexander Graham Bell, who recommended Sullivan, a formerly blind recent graduate of the Perkins Institution in Boston, to be Keller's teacher and governess.

Willful and creative herself, Sullivan descended on Keller with a mixture of strong discipline and imaginative lessons that caught the unruly young girl off-guard. Keller's famous breakthrough at the water pump happened a mere two weeks after Sullivan came to live with the family. Later, Keller always celebrated March 3, 1887, the day the woman she called simply "Teacher" arrived, as "my soul's birthday." Theirs was an astonishing lifelong collaboration that raised fascinating questions about dependence, need, and communication.

After learning to read by mastering the Braille alphabet (a system of raised dots readable by touch), Keller began the slow process of learning to speak and to lip-read by placing her fingers on the lips and throat of the speaker while the words were spelled out in her hand. At fourteen, she attended a school for the deaf in New York City; at sixteen, she went to the Cambridge School for Young Ladies in Massachusetts; at twenty, she entered Radcliffe College, graduating cum laude in 1904, having mastered several more languages. With the publication of her autobiography in 1903, she became a celebrity. Keller lectured around the world, primarily on behalf of the American Foundation for the Blind, championing improved conditions and more humane treatment for blind and deaf people.

Sullivan died in 1936. As a way of adjusting to life without Teacher, Keller went to Japan with her secretary on a lecture tour and gave nearly one hundred speeches. She kept a journal for therapeutic reasons and to vindicate herself and Sullivan, whom people had accused for years of unduly influencing and enhancing Keller's thoughts and work. "People will see that I have a personality, not gifted, but my own," she wrote in *Helen Keller's Journal*, which was published in 1938 and which put to rest the question of her authenticity.

In 1964, Keller was awarded the Presidential Medal of Freedom. Looking back on her childhood, she wrote, "Everything has its wonders, even darkness and silence, and I learn, whatever state I may be in, therein to be content."

Opposite: Helen Keller. **Below:** Coco Chanel in 1931. **Right:** Helen Keller communicates with her lifelong companion and teacher, Annie Sullivan.

Gabrielle "Coco" Chanel
fashion designer (1883–1971)

The reigning queen of fashion for nearly six decades, Parisian designer Coco Chanel liberated turn-of-the-century women from corsets and plumage with her simple, classic look that has yet to go out of style. Her popular designs—including the famous "little black dress," cardigan suits with braided collars, and casual jersey sweaters—were smart, comfortable, and affordable for working women. "In order to be irreplaceable one must always be different," she said.

After her mother's death when Gabrielle was six years old, her father abandoned her and her two sisters. Raised in an orphanage, she was sent at age seventeen to a convent in Moulins, France, where she learned to sew. While she was working as an assistant in a clothing shop frequented by the wealthy residents of nearby castles, Chanel's quality alteration work quickly attracted a loyal clientele. Inspired by the jersey smocks she wore in the convent, Chanel began to create sweaters and blazers in comfortable knit fabrics. In 1913, she opened her own

hems rose, she introduced the little black dress paired with two-tone shoes. In 1922, she developed her most successful and enduring creation: the perfume Chanel No. 5.

She counted many artists among her friends, hosting Russian composer Igor Stravinsky when he emigrated to France, financing dance impresario Sergei Diaghilev's revival of *The Rite of Spring*, and designing costumes for French playwright Jean Cocteau's production of *Antigone*, which also featured backdrops by Pablo Picasso. Sophisticated and chic, Chanel had become a cultural icon in France.

Chanel did not fare as well during World War II. She closed her clothing shops in 1939 and remained in Paris throughout most of the war, moving to Switzerland in 1944. Ten years later, at the age of seventy-one, Chanel came out of retirement and reopened her shop in Paris. Her new ideas included the timeless braid-trimmed suits in jersey and tweed, and the leather handbag bearing her signature back-to-back "C" on the clasp. "When I can no longer create anything, I'll be done for," she explained.

boutique in Deauville, an affluent seaside resort in Normandy. Her designs introduced a sporty casualness coveted by the vacationing rich, incorporating horse-racing themes and English sailor motifs. She then expanded to a shop in Paris, where she firmly established her classically elegant style.

The outbreak of World War I soon brought a period of scarcity. Metal to be used for the stays of corsets was unavailable, and the shortage of other materials dictated simpler lines, less fabric, and shorter hems. Chanel's visionary designs fit the bill; her business did well during the war and flourished during the Roaring Twenties.

In the early 1920s, Chanel's glamorous look captured the youthful spirit that fashion, art, and society were embracing. She offered sleeveless evening gowns, and as waists dropped and

Georgia O'Keeffe
artist (1887–1986)

*a*merican artist Georgia O'Keeffe's gorgeous paintings of flowers, desert landscapes, and city skylines defy categorization yet are instantly recognizable the world over. Both realistic and abstract, her paintings are testimony to her unique vision. "I said to myself—I'll paint what I see—what the flower is to me," she wrote, "but I'll paint it big and they will be surprised into taking time to look at it—I will make even busy New Yorkers take time to see what I see of flowers." Throughout a lifetime that spanned nearly a century, critics, art collectors, and just plain folks were captivated by what she saw.

O'Keeffe's original style and remarkable talent established her as one of the greatest artists of the twentieth century.

Certain even as a young girl in Sun Prairie, Wisconsin, that she wanted to be a painter, O'Keeffe studied art in Chicago and New York, and then became a freelance commercial artist in Chicago until a bad case of the measles sent her home to recuperate with her parents, then living in Virginia. She halfheartedly enrolled in a drawing course at the University of Virginia, where she discovered the fascinating abstract theories of Arthur Wesley Dow—what O'Keeffe described as "filling space in a beautiful way." In 1914, she returned to New York to study under Dow himself at Columbia University.

Inspired to follow her creative notions, O'Keeffe decided to develop her own organic style from scratch. Beginning with watercolors and pulling back to black-and-white charcoal

Above: Georgia O'Keeffe shows her painting *Pelvis, Red and Yellow.*

sketches, O'Keeffe struggled to express the exact essence of her emotions in abstract shapes. "The meaning of a word—to me—is not as exact as the meaning of a color," she wrote. "Color and shapes make a more definite statement than words."

In 1916, O'Keeffe sent some sketches to a friend in New York, who showed them to Alfred Stieglitz, a famous photographer and modern art patron. Without O'Keeffe's knowledge, Stieglitz exhibited her drawings at his cutting-edge gallery, known as 291, to critical acclaim and great public interest. She moved to New York to be with the much-older Stieglitz in 1918; they married in 1924. Over the years, Stieglitz took more than three hundred portraits of O'Keeffe, and he exhibited her work almost every year until his death in 1946.

Throughout the 1920s, O'Keeffe created a beautiful series of lush, erotic, larger-than-life paintings of flowers. But by 1929, she had become unhappy in the congested city of New York. That spring, she traveled to Taos, New Mexico, and discovered her psychic home. Stunned by the desert landscape and the light, she never tired of trying to capture them on canvas. She lived six months of each year in New Mexico and moved permanently to Abiquiu, New Mexico, when her husband died.

Writing to James Johnson Sweeney, a curator who was organizing an exhibition of her work at the Museum of Modern Art in New York, in 1945, O'Keeffe described her contribution to American art this way: "I should add that I think that I am one of the few who gives our country any voice of its own—I claim no credit—it is only that I have seen with my own eye and that I couldn't help seeing with my own eye."

Marian Anderson
singer (1902–1993)

On Easter Sunday in 1939, African-American contralto Marian Anderson sang beautifully on the steps of the Lincoln Memorial before an enthusiastic crowd of seventy-five thousand people. Millions more heard her rich voice over the radio.

This historic concert almost didn't take place. After causing a sensation in Europe—conductor Arturo Toscanini told her,

AMAZING GRACE

"Yours is a voice such as one hears once in a hundred years"—Anderson had returned home to the United States to continue her stellar career. When she tried to book Constitution Hall in Washington, D.C., she was refused permission by the concert hall's owners, the Daughters of the American Revolution (DAR), who barred blacks from performing or attending events there. First Lady Eleanor Roosevelt resigned her membership from the DAR immediately in protest and arranged for Anderson's outdoor triumph. "If you are all right on the inside, you don't have to worry about things like that," Anderson later said.

Below: Marian Anderson returns to the scene of her triumph to perform at the memorial service for former Secretary of the Interior Harold Ickes, who helped arrange her historic 1939 Lincoln Memorial concert. **Opposite:** Marian Anderson.

A member of her Philadelphia church choir as a child, Anderson also gave solo concerts for a fee of five dollars. Billed as "Baby Contralto," she was able to earn much-needed money for her close-knit family. Her father bought young Marian a piano but was unable to afford lessons, so she taught herself to play well enough to accompany herself.

In high school, Anderson's talent was nurtured in the chorus, and upon graduation she applied to a Philadelphia music school. Again, racism blocked her path; she was denied entry. "It's like a hair across your cheek," Anderson said about bigotry. "You can't see it, you can't find it with your fingers, but you keep brushing at it because the feel of it is irritating."

Anderson decided to study voice privately with Giuseppe Boghetti, who focused on her breathing technique and introduced her to songs by classical composers. Sponsored by black organizations, she toured the United States, giving concerts at black churches and colleges. After winning first prize in a competition in 1925, Anderson was invited to appear with the New York Philharmonic; her performance was well-received. She then won a fellowship to study in Germany, and from 1930 to 1935 she gave concerts throughout Europe, where audiences were more receptive to performers of all races.

Returning to the United States in 1935, she gave an outstanding performance at New York's Town Hall. Her amazing range and pure vocal quality were without peer. Though still unwelcome in the world's opera houses, Anderson gave about seventy recitals a year. She finally shattered the color barrier in 1955: singing the role of Ulrica in Verdi's *Un Ballo in Maschera*, Anderson was the first black person to perform at the Metropolitan Opera. She sang at the inaugurations of Presidents Eisenhower and Kennedy and was appointed an ambassador to the United Nations in 1958. After an extensive farewell concert tour, Anderson retired in 1965.

Anderson supported the careers of young singers through cash scholarships, although she was characteristically modest. "I think that those that came after me deserve a great deal of credit for what they have achieved," she said. "I don't feel that I am responsible for any of it, because if they didn't have it in them, they wouldn't be able to get it out."

19

Wilma Rudolph

athlete (1940–1994)

Above: Wilma Rudolph, known as "La Gazelle" because of her speed and fluid running style, wins one of her three gold medals at the 1960 Olympics. **Opposite:** Barbra Streisand not only directed but also starred with Nick Nolte in *The Prince of Tides*.

Being unable to walk without a brace never slowed down Wilma Rudolph. After a series of childhood illnesses, she had lost the use of her left leg. "The doctors told me I would never walk," she said, "but my mother told me I would, so I believed my mother." With the loving support of her big family (she was the twentieth out of twenty-two children) and sheer determination, she learned not only to walk but to run. In 1960, Rudolph made history as the first American woman to win three gold medals in track and field in a single Olympiad.

The daughter of a railroad porter and a domestic worker, Rudolph grew up in the segregated town of Clarksville, Tennessee. Twice a week, her mother drove her fifty miles (80km) for physical therapy at the only area hospital open to black people; back home, she and the other children constantly massaged and exercised young Wilma's leg. When she was eight, Rudolph was strong enough to walk without her brace; by the age of eleven, she discarded her orthopedic shoe and turned to sports.

As a member of her high school basketball team, Rudolph was noticed for her athletic promise by Ed Temple, the Tennessee State University track coach. He persuaded her to switch to track, and she began training with him at the age of fourteen. "I loved the feeling of freedom in running, the fresh air, the feeling that the only person I'm really competing with is me," she wrote in her 1977 autobiography, *Wilma*. Rudolph never lost a race in four seasons of high school track. At sixteen, she was the youngest member of the bronze-medal-winning 1956 U.S. Olympic track and field team. She continued to train with Temple when she enrolled at the university in 1957.

At the 1960 Olympics, held in Rome, Rudolph, dubbed "La Gazelle" by the French press, reached new heights. She won the one-hundred-meter dash (tying the world record) and the two-hundred-meter dash (setting a new world record), and brought her four-hundred-meter relay team from behind to win. Her hometown threw her a victory parade; upon her insistence, it was a racially integrated event, the first ever held there.

When Rudolph graduated from Tennessee State in 1963, she retired from amateur athletics, unwilling to risk defeat in the 1964 Olympics. She dedicated her life to young people, as a schoolteacher, a coach, and a mother raising four children. She helped to open and run several inner-city sports clinics, and in 1982 started the Wilma Rudolph Foundation in Indianapolis, Indiana, dedicated to promoting amateur athletics. "I would be very disappointed if I were only remembered as a runner because I feel that my contribution to the youth of America has far exceeded the woman who was the Olympic champion," she said. Rudolph was just fifty-four when she died from a malignant brain tumor.

Barbra Streisand

singer, actor, director, and producer (1942–)

*T*he incomparable Barbra Streisand—she of glorious voice, impeccable comedic timing, and uncompromising artistic vision—is an artist with an amazingly broad range of talent. Even she finds it hard to categorize herself, saying: "I am simple, complex, generous, selfish, unattractive, beautiful, lazy, and driven." With twenty-one top-ten albums, she has had more gold records than any other solo performer. She has won seven Grammy awards, an Emmy, an Oscar for best actress, and a Tony award as "star of the decade" (for the 1960s). The prolific Streisand is firmly established as one of the century's greatest all-around entertainers.

Brooklyn-born Streisand started out singing in Greenwich Village coffee houses, where she was spotted by Broadway producer David Merrick. In 1962, he cast her in the minor role of Miss Marmelstein in *I Can Get It For You Wholesale*; she stole the show. Next, she starred as Fanny Brice in the Broadway musical *Funny Girl* and became a star. Streisand reprised her role in the film version of *Funny Girl* and was awarded the 1969 best actress Oscar, a tribute she shared with Katharine Hepburn.

After building an enormous following through her hit records, television specials, and popular films, such as *On a Clear Day You Can See Forever*, *The Way We Were*, and *A Star is Born*, Streisand took a huge professional risk. In 1981, with *Yentl*, she became the first woman to direct, produce, write, and star in a feature film. Although it produced a best-selling soundtrack, critics either loved the film or hated it, and Streisand was hammered for daring to wield so much power. "If a man wants to get it right, he's looked up to and respected," she pointed out. "If a woman wants to get it right, she's difficult or impossible. If he acts, produces, and directs, he's called multitalented. If she does the same thing, she's called vain and egotistical." In 1991, her epic romance *The Prince of Tides* won over critics and audiences alike, although she was overlooked for a directing nomination

AMAZING GRACE

by the Academy. She produced, directed, and starred in 1996's *The Mirror Has Two Faces*, in which her complex character was reminiscent of the endearingly awkward women of her early films.

A compulsive perfectionist with performance phobia, Streisand did not sing live for decades. Her desire to support progressive causes finally outweighed her severe stage fright, and in the late 1980's she gave an outdoor concert to benefit environmental groups and performed at a benefit for presidential candidate and friend Bill Clinton. She was finally coaxed back to the concert circuit with a classy sold-out tour in 1994. Her exquisite voice, nuanced interpretations, and breathtaking performances surpassed everyone's high expectations.

Passionate and obsessive about her work, Streisand defends her style: "You know, the audience buys my work because I control it, *because* I am a perfectionist, because I care deeply."

Joni Mitchell
singer and songwriter (1943–)

Above: Joni Mitchell, beloved by fans and fellow musicians alike for her artistry and originality, performs at a 1979 concert.
Opposite: Streisand mesmerizes the audience in Auburn Hills, Michigan, a stop on her 1994 sold-out tour, which was her first in decades.

Joni Mitchell has been called the most influential singer-songwriter of her generation. She is revered by an amazing array of popular musicians and artists and inspires unshakable devotion in her fans. Innovative, bold, and frank, Mitchell ignores the demands of the market to stay true to her personal vision of what her music should be.

Born Roberta Joan Anderson, she grew up as an only child in Saskatoon, Saskatchewan, Canada. A promising athlete, she was stricken with polio at the age of nine and turned to the arts during her long convalescence. She took piano lessons and taught herself to play guitar. She attended art school in Calgary before moving to Toronto, where she established herself in the local folk music scene and met folk singer Chuck Mitchell, to whom she was briefly married. She later settled in California.

Even in the early years of her recording career, which began in 1968, it was clear that Mitchell possessed extraordinary talent: her melodies are graceful, her lyrics poetic, her arrangements engaging, and her voice versatile. An accomplished painter, Mitchell has created the art for most of her album covers.

In her first albums—*Joni Mitchell*, *Clouds*, *Ladies of the Canyon*, *Blue*, and *For the Roses*—Mitchell chose a spare and lean folk sound, accompanying herself on guitar or piano. Her themes were the intimate terrain of relationships, although she has always bristled at her work being called "confessional." "The point is not to confess," she said. "I've always used the songwriting process as a self-analysis of sorts." These early recordings sold well and gained her a loyal following. *Blue*, with its moody, haunting songs, became a classic, a standard by which the work of Mitchell—and other artists—would come to be measured.

On *Court and Spark*, released in 1974, she added other instruments and developed more elaborate arrangements. Its jazz-inflected sound was a hint of new directions to come. With subsequent albums, she took her work in a more inventive and noncommercial direction, experimenting with jazz, world music rhythms, and even classical orchestration. *The Hissing of Summer*

AMAZING GRACE

Lawns, Don Juan's Reckless Daughter, Dog Eat Dog, and *Mingus* (a collaboration with jazz composer and bassist Charles Mingus) got cold receptions from critics and were commercially unsuccessful. Having won two Grammys in the early 1970s, Mitchell was ignored by the Academy for the next twenty years as she carved out her own artistic path. With her 1994 Grammy for *Turbulent Indigo*, critics revisited her previous works and came to view them as daring and profoundly influential for future songwriters.

Mitchell's themes broadened as well. Although ideas of social justice were evident as early as 1970, with "Big Yellow Taxi" ("They paved paradise / And put up a parking lot"), her later work is more noticeably tinged with biting social critique. She skewers consumerism, hypocrisy, mediocrity, and fundamental-ism of any sort. Her early fans remain devoted to her, and she enjoys a new generation of fans who, having been exposed to a host of Mitchell-inspired artists, have gradually discovered the original article.

Martina Navratilova
athlete (1956–)

Above: Martina Navratilova's serve often reached 90 miles an hour (140kph); here she follows through at the 1993 U.S. Open.
Opposite: Joni Mitchell in 1968.

ennis great Martina Navratilova loves to win. "Whoever said, 'It's not whether you win or lose that counts,' probably lost," she once quipped. Dominating the sport throughout the 1980s, she won often and decisively, taking home more singles titles than any other player, male or female. With her power-serve-and-volley game, superb fitness, and hall-mark candor, Navratilova revolutionized tennis; many consider her the best female athlete of the century.

"The moment I stepped onto that crunchy red clay," she wrote in her 1985 autobiography, *Martina*, "felt the grit under my sneakers, felt the joy of smacking the ball over the net, I knew I was in the right place." A natural athlete, Navratilova hit the ski slopes at age two in her native Czechoslovakia. By the age of six, she was playing tennis seriously. Encouraged by her parents, who were tennis administrators for the Communist government, Navratilova was a national champion at the age of fourteen.

In 1973, competing in a United States Tennis Association tour, Navratilova tasted freedom and junk food for the first time and loved them both. She played against Chris Evert (and lost) in the first-ever match of what was to become a legendary rivalry and friendship. Chafing under the restrictive interference of her government, in 1975 she defected after the U.S. Open tournament. Although she was now without family or country (she became a U.S. citizen in 1981), she was free to make her own decisions, and nineteen-year-old Navratilova's career took off. In 1976, she won her first Wimbledon title in a doubles match with Evert; in 1978, she earned her first Wimbledon singles title, ironically, against Evert. Over the next fifteen years, the two friends would continu-ally challenge each other to play their best tennis.

A powerhouse of strength, the left-handed Navratilova threw herself into fitness training, a strict diet, and weightlifting, a routine that changed the shape of her muscles and redefined women's athleticism. She aggressively rushed the net, finishing off her opponents with ninety-mile-an-hour (140 kph) serves, lightning reflexes, and devastating volleys. Navratilova was ranked number one seven times in her career. She garnered more singles (167) and doubles (165) titles than any other woman, won a record seventy-four straight singles matches, and holds a record nine Wimbledon singles titles. One of the best grass court players ever, Navratilova loved competing at Wimbledon. After her final match there in 1994, she plucked a few blades of grass from Centre Court and stuck them in her pocket.

Off the court, Navratilova caused a stir as the first open lesbian in women's tennis. She handled the pressure and the media's homophobia with grace and humor. "Do you think the tennis ball is afraid of me because I'm gay and that's why I hit it better?" she joked. "Giving my best doesn't have anything to do with being gay or not. I don't think homosexuality has a patent on excellence." She is an effective spokesperson for the gay and lesbian community and a staunch supporter of women's rights.

On November 15, 1994, Navratilova played her final singles match, in the Virginia Slims tournament, losing to Gabriela Sabatini at Madison Square Garden. It hardly mattered; the audience was clearly in her court. A red-and-gold banner bearing her name was raised to the roof to the strains of Tina Turner's "Simply the Best."

Alice Walker
writer and poet (1944–)

A brilliant novelist, essayist, and poet, Alice Walker speaks from the heart and cuts right to the hearts of her readers with writing that is exquisitely crafted and unflinchingly honest. A small, soft-spoken woman who exudes wisdom and strength, Walker has created some of the most powerful works of the twentieth century.

Throughout her nineteen books, one of Walker's consistent themes is personal responsibility to oneself, other creatures, and the planet. "I believe in the soul," she wrote in 1988. "Furthermore, I believe that it is prompt accountability for one's choices, a willing acceptance of responsibility of one's thoughts, behavior and actions, that makes it powerful. The white man's oppression of me will never excuse my oppression of you, whether you are man, woman, child, animal or tree, because the self that I prize refuses to be owned by him. Or by anyone."

Walker grew up the youngest of eight children in a poor family in Eatonton, Georgia. When she was eight years old, she was blinded in one eye when one of her brothers shot her with a BB gun. A scholarship for the "handicapped" from the state of Georgia enabled her to attend Spelman College, and she later transferred to Sarah Lawrence College. She traveled to Africa during her senior year and returned distraught over an unplanned pregnancy. Frantic and suicidal, she had an abortion. Walker then wrote compulsively about suicide, love, and Africa, producing her first volume of poetry, *Once*, which was published three years later, in 1968.

Walker's poetry—spare, evocative, and powerful—speaks volumes in a few words. She writes: "Be nobody's darling; / Be an outcast. / Qualified to live / Among your dead." In another poem, she urges: "Expect nothing. Live frugally / on surprise."

Her books, including two collections of essays, *In Search of Our Mothers' Gardens* and *Living By the Word*; the more recent novels, *The Temple of My Familiar* and *Possessing the Secret of Joy*; and non-fiction books, *The Same River Twice: Honoring the Difficult* and *Anything We Love Can Be Saved: A Writer's Activism*, have sold nearly ten million copies and have been translated into more than two dozen languages. Walker is a rare writer who sees the world whole and, through her deeply spiritual and provocative writings, challenges us to do the same.

Maya Lin
architect (1960–)

*a*s an architecture student at Yale University, Maya Lin entered a 1981 nationwide design competition for a memorial honoring Vietnam veterans, "knowing full well it wouldn't be chosen," she said, "because it wasn't a politically glorified statement about war." However, a blue-ribbon panel did select Lin's entry over more than fourteen hundred others, and, at just twenty-one years old, she created one of the most provocative public monuments in history.

Lin's idea was to focus on the tragedy of the lives lost in the war. When she visited the site, she envisioned a shiny, black wall that would gradually slope upward as visitors descend down to a vertex; a wall that would bear the names of the 57,661 Americans who died in the war, listed by the years of their deaths. "The memorial is composed not as an unchanging monument," she wrote, "but as a moving composition to be understood as we move into and out of it."

When Lin's plan was unveiled, a small, powerful group of detractors—made up of some veterans, conservative politicians, and right-wing commentators—viciously castigated the artist and labeled her design "a scar," "a black hole," and "dishonorable." Withstanding racist and personal attacks, young Lin forcefully defended the spatial and artistic integrity of the memorial. In the

Above: Alice Walker in 1991. **Opposite:** Navratilova manages a smile after a heartbreaking defeat in 1985 by her rival and friend Chris Evert.

She met and married civil rights lawyer Melvyn Leventhal, and they moved to Mississippi; she worked in the civil rights movement, registering black voters and developing educational materials for Head Start programs. Their daughter, Rebecca, was born in 1969, three days after the completion of Walker's first novel, *The Third Life of Grange Copeland*.

Walker eventually divorced Leventhal and settled in northern California, where she wrote her best-known novel, *The Color Purple*, winner of the American Book Award and the Pulitzer Prize for fiction. The story of Celie, a girl who survives physical, sexual, and emotional abuse by men through her relationships with women, the novel is written in the form of letters from Celie to God, and later between Celie and her sister. Poignant and visionary, *The Color Purple* is ultimately a story of beauty, hope, and the strength and community of black women.

studio. She inherited her parents' critical eye and their taste for a "clean aesthetic."

Lin has designed several other compelling pieces, including the Civil Rights Memorial in Montgomery, Alabama. Inspired by the words of Martin Luther King, Jr., "...until justice rolls down like waters and righteousness like a mighty stream," Lin created a waterfall that cascades onto a flat, round surface and rolls gently over its sides. Carved into the stone surface is a chronological listing of civil rights movement milestones; the names of those who died in the struggle are intertwined with political acts so that viewers absorb how people changed history.

"An artist fights to retain the integrity of a work so that it remains a strong, clear vision," Lin said. "Art is and should be the act of an individual willing to say something new, something not quite familiar."

Above: Maya Lin proudly displays her controversial design for the Vietnam Veterans Memorial.

end, the wall was built as Lin had planned it, although a statue of soldiers and an American flag were placed at the entrance to the memorial.

Dedicated on Veterans Day 1982, the powerfully stark Vietnam Veterans Memorial is the most visited National Park Service site in Washington, D.C., and has become a symbol of national healing. Visitors are stunned by the impact of the names; many search for the names of their loved ones, leaving flowers, messages, and mementos. "It's only when you accept the pain, it's only when you accept the death, that you can then come away from it," Lin explained. "And literally as you read a name, or touch a name, the pain will come out—and I really did mean for people to cry. Then you can of your own power turn around and walk back up into the light, into the present."

The daughter of Chinese immigrants, Lin grew up in Athens, Ohio, where her parents taught at Ohio University. Her father was a fine-arts professor; young Maya played in the department's

Meryl Streep
actor (1949–)

With her extraordinary versatility, impressive technique, and astonishing emotional range, Meryl Streep swept Hollywood off its feet in the late 1970s and has remained one of the most accomplished actors of our time. Nominated for ten Oscars and the winner of two, she has crafted a career playing an incredible assortment of complex women. Off-screen, Streep has demonstrated quite a range as well—as wife, mother, activist, and advocate for improving the status of women in Hollywood.

The only child of a well-to-do family in Madison, New Jersey, Streep graduated in 1971 from Vassar College with a degree in drama and costume design and earned a master's in fine arts from the Yale School of Drama in 1975. After being consistently lauded as a leading actor with New York's prestigious Public Theater, in 1977 she appeared in her first film, *Julia*. The

Streep created memorable characters in such diverse films as *Silkwood*, *Falling in Love*, *Out of Africa*, and *A Cry in the Dark*.

An actor with impeccable timing, Streep next frolicked in a string of comedies, including *She-Devil* and *Postcards From the Edge*, before returning to drama. At an age when leading roles for women are scarce, Streep continues to land challenging parts.

In 1978, Streep married sculptor Don Gummer; they are raising four children. A devoted mother, Streep has sidestepped the fast-paced Hollywood life and is mindful of her children as she chooses her roles. "Grabbing the cold gold at the Oscars was great," she said. "But it didn't come close to being handed my first-born—or my fourth-born for that matter." She has passed on roles that would have taken her too far away from her kids or for too long. In her mid-forties, she chose to ride white-water rapids in the action adventure film *The River Wild* to model fearlessness for her children.

"Acting is being susceptible to what is around you, and it's letting it all come in," said Streep. "Acting is a clearing away of everything except what you want and need—and it's wonderful in that way. And when it's right, you're lost in the moment."

Above: Meryl Streep in 1994. **Below:** Streep's searing portrayal of a Holocaust survivor in the 1982 film *Sophie's Choice* won her a best actress Oscar.

following year she was nominated for an Academy Award for her supporting role in *The Deer Hunter* and won an Emmy for her performance in the miniseries *Holocaust*. By 1979, Streep was all over the big screen—as the seductress in *The Seduction of Joe Tynan*, the lesbian ex-wife in Woody Allen's *Manhattan*, and the absentee mother in *Kramer vs. Kramer*, her first Oscar-winning performance. Rewriting key *Kramer vs. Kramer* scenes to transform her stereotypical character into a realistic, complicated woman, Streep began a pattern of shaping her characters into well-rounded, nuanced women rarely portrayed on-screen.

Throughout the 1980s, Streep's virtuoso performances dominated the box office. After starring in *The French Lieutenant's Woman* (1981), she won the best actress Oscar for her unforgettable tour de force as a Polish Holocaust survivor in *Sophie's Choice*. Her ability to master any accent and to inhabit characters of any background and era is remarkable. "The great gift of human beings is that we have the power of empathy," she said.

29

AMAZING GRACE

Chapter

2

PIONEERING SPIRIT

Marie Curie, chemist and physicist

Jane Addams, reformer

Luisa Capetillo, activist

Julia Morgan, architect

Margaret Mead, anthropologist

Amelia Earhart, aviator

Charlayne Hunter-Gault, journalist

Valentina Tereshkova, cosmonaut

Twyla Tharp, choreographer and dancer

Shirley Chisholm, politician

Geraldine Ferraro, politician

Ann Bancroft, polar explorer

Cynthia Cooper, athlete

With equal parts courage, vision, and endurance, these women forged their ways into unfamiliar territory and made it their own. Their bravery and their generosity in marking the trail have allowed those who followed to imagine new possibilities.

Amelia Earhart

Margaret Mead

Charlayne Hunter-Gault

Geraldine Ferraro

Jane Addams

Julia Morgan

Ann Bancroft

Valentina Tereshkova

Shirley Chisholm

Marie Curie
chemist and physicist (1867–1934)

At the turn of the century, many physicists believed that science had explained everything about the physical universe and that their only remaining task was to improve their measurements. Imagine their surprise when Marie Curie, the first world-famous woman scientist, discovered several new elements and captured a new force of nature, which she called radioactivity. Biographer Mollie Kellor asserts that "this tiny woman with her decigram of radium turned the world upside down, forever changing the way we look at, understand, and use our environment."

Born Marya Sklowdoska into a family of teachers in Warsaw, Poland, she was a brilliant student, graduating at the top of her high school class at just fifteen. The country was under Russian occupation, however, and women were barred from attending universities. After six years as a governess, Marya left for France, changing her first name to Marie. Living out the classic scenario of a starving student in a sixth-floor garret, she enrolled at the Sorbonne and happily earned degrees in physics and mathematics in rapid succession, despite a shaky grasp of French.

There she met Pierre Curie, an accomplished physicist, and the two scientists were immediately inseparable. Their marriage in 1895 created one of the most significant scientific partnerships in history. The Curies worked together day and night and hardly missed a moment in the laboratory, even when their daughter Irène was born. Remarkably, Pierre's father moved in with them to care for Irène and, later, her sister, Eve, when Marie returned to work.

Curie's brilliant doctoral thesis explored the source of mysterious rays given off by uranium ores. She hypothesized that an unknown, new element was probably responsible. Intrigued by her theory, Pierre Curie gave up his own research to join his wife's quest. To obtain a minuscule sample of this radioactive material, the Curies processed tons of a mineral called pitchblende. The only location large enough for their work was an abandoned shed with poor heating and ventilation, and there the Curies made their most important discoveries: two new radioactive elements, which they named polonium (in honor of Curie's beloved native land) and radium. The Curies were awarded the 1903 Nobel Prize in physics for "their joint researches on the radiation phenomena." In 1911, Marie Curie won her second Nobel Prize, this time in chemistry, for proving the existence of radium.

The Curies decided not to patent their work, preferring to keep their research in a purer realm. This decision condemned them to a lifetime of woefully inadequate and unsafe laboratory facilities. Unaware of its poisonous properties, the Curies handled radioactive material for years without protection. Almost one hundred years later, their lab notebooks are still wildly radioactive.

In 1906, tragedy struck when Pierre Curie stepped in front of a horse-drawn carriage and was killed. Devastated, Marie Curie nonetheless committed herself to completing their research on her own. She assumed her husband's professorship at the Sorbonne, ran its laboratory, and, with her daughter Irène, developed X-rays as a medical tool.

Curie's health gradually failed from the effects of long-term exposure to radiation. Her precious radium, which had offered the first ray of hope for cancer patients, ironically was responsible for her death from leukemia.

Below: Marie Curie made some of her most complex
discoveries in this spare and simple laboratory.
Opposite: Marie Curie in 1921.

33

PIONEERING SPIRIT

Jane Addams

reformer (1860–1935)

Best known as the mother of the settlement house movement in the United States, Jane Addams was also a suffrage leader, an advocate for poor people, a founder of the American Civil Liberties Union, a pacifist, and the first woman to win the Nobel Peace Prize. Fiercely independent, Addams held fast to her beliefs, no matter how controversial, and threw herself headlong into social justice causes. In her lifetime, she was called "America's most useful citizen," the nation's "most admired woman," and "the most dangerous woman in America."

Addams grew up in a prosperous family in Illinois. Her mother died when Jane was two; her father, a reform-minded, abolitionist businessman and politician, was a huge influence on his daughter, who grew up determined, she wrote, "to improve the world's way of living."

In 1888, she found her mission and opened Hull House, one of the country's first settlement houses. In an era when immigrants living in poverty were despised and feared, Addams and her friend Ellen Gates Starr took over a rundown mansion in the heart of the tenement district in Chicago to live among the people they served—poor immigrants from Greece, Italy, Russia, Germany, Sicily, and many other countries. They stayed for forty-six years.

Hull House started out addressing the immediate needs of the community—providing job training and education, entertainment, lectures, recreation, a playground, and nursery care. Within four years, Addams and the small group of extraordinary women and men who lived with her at Hull House were serving two thousand people each week. Eventually, Hull House expanded to include thirteen buildings around the original site, and a summer campground near Lake Geneva, Wisconsin.

Exposure to the deplorable living conditions of the poor inspired Addams and her coworkers to move beyond social service. They became activists on the local and state levels, campaigning to end sweatshop conditions, ban child labor, mobilize support for labor unions, create legal protections for immigrants, pass housing regulations, and establish the first juvenile court in the nation. "Action is indeed the sole medium of expression for ethics," she later reflected.

Addams lectured widely and wrote a dozen books, including two memoirs. An early proponent of cultural understanding and valuing diversity, she emphasized community responsibility in solving the problems of urban life. Some of Chicago's upper class, who had praised her work as "Christian charity," were less appreciative when Addams started trying to change the conditions of the poor instead of just ministering to them.

During World War I, Addams was instrumental in organizing an international peace movement. After the United States entered the war in 1917, she was denounced for her pacifism and booted out of the Daughters of the American Revolution. In 1919, she was elected the first president of the Women's International League for Peace and Freedom (WILPF), a post she held until her death. In 1931, she won the Nobel Peace Prize; she donated the prize money to Hull House and WILPF, ever generous and committed to the causes she fought for all her life.

Below: Jane Addams, founder of Hull House and the settlement movement, surrounded by children. **Opposite:** Addams in 1914.

Luisa Capetillo
activist (1879–1922)

In her short lifetime, revolutionary Luisa Capetillo organized labor strikes, marched for women's suffrage, and wrote countless articles about the exploitation of women and workers, but she is more often remembered as the first woman in her country to wear pants in public.

As Capetillo was coming of age, her hometown of Arecibo, Puerto Rico, was in the throes of tremendous change. Laborers left farms for new factory jobs created by American industry, only to find themselves making less money and leading more difficult lives. Capetillo worked ten- to twelve-hour shifts in factories, earning as little as three cents a day. With little formal schooling available, she educated herself, and was the only woman in the factories who could read. A fierce advocate for workers' rights, she lobbied for better pay, believing that decent wages would improve employee morale, diminish domestic violence, and offer a brighter future for the workers' children. Capetillo also inspired factory and sugar plantation workers to rebel against their conditions.

After taking part in a tobacco workers' strike in 1907, Capetillo became a leader in the working-class struggle—an extraordinary feat for a woman of her time. She joined the Federation of Free Workers and in 1910 became a reporter for the organization's newspaper. That same year she founded her own newspaper, *La Mujer* (The Woman), to publicize and politicize women's issues.

A radical visionary, Capetillo was a passionate and prolific writer. She condemned the exploitation of workers; denounced the oppression of women, particularly through the institution of marriage, which she considered slavery; and promoted women's suffrage and liberation, free love, and libertarian socialism. Her 1910 article "La humanidad en el futuro" (Humanity in the Future) imagined a fully realized utopian society, and her 1911 book titled *Mi opinión sobre las libertades, derechos y deberes de la mujer como compañera, madre y ser independiente* ("My Opinion on the Freedoms, Rights and Duties of the Woman as Companion, Mother and as an Independent Being") is considered Puerto Rico's first women's rights manifesto. Capetillo writes in the preface, "I believe nothing impossible; I do not wonder about any moment or discovery; that is why I do not find any idea utopian. The essential thing is to put it into practice. To begin!"

Beginning in 1912, Capetillo spent several years organizing for labor reform in New York and Florida (which were centers of anarchist and socialist activity for tobacco industry workers) and finally Cuba, fighting for literacy and better working conditions. Always eager to shatter social conventions, Capetillo had three children without marrying their father, and in 1915, she was arrested on the street in Cuba for "instigating public disorder" by wearing men's clothing. When she was deported from Cuba for her political activity, she returned to Puerto Rico and, despite public disapproval, continued to cross dress.

Capetillo died of tuberculosis at the age of forty-two, leaving a legacy of visionary and inspiring ideas that scholars and activists are just starting to rediscover.

Julia Morgan
architect (1872–1957)

In an era when girls and women were encouraged to dream of living in a castle, architect Julia Morgan was building one. In 1919, publishing magnate William Randolph Hearst commissioned Morgan to create the castle at San Simeon, which remains one of the most famous and majestic twentieth-century buildings. In the exclusively male world of architecture, the prolific Morgan carved out her own path and left an exquisite legacy of more than seven hundred buildings.

Sickly as a child and painfully shy as an adult, Morgan allowed her work to speak for her. As the first woman enrolled in the College of Engineering of the University of California at Berkeley, Morgan met influential architect Bernard Maybeck, who encouraged her to go on to attend his alma mater, the Ecole des Beaux-Arts in Paris. Morgan went to Paris in 1896 but was denied admission because of her gender. When she won a blind design competition, however, two years later, the school was forced to grant Morgan admission. In 1902, she became its first woman graduate, and upon returning to the United States, she became the first woman to be granted an architecture license by the state of California.

She began her career in the offices of San Francisco architect John Galen Howard, who was designing a master building plan for the University of California, commissioned by philanthropist Phoebe Apperson Hearst. Morgan's clear talent and the decorative details she created on two university buildings immediately impressed Hearst, who became her patron. Morgan opened her own office in San Francisco in 1904 and, over the years, employed a number of women architects and draftspeople, enrolling them in her European-style apprentice system.

With high-visibility early commissions like the Mission-style bell tower at Mills College, Morgan quickly built up a significant business. Her style was eclectic, but she was increasingly drawn to the Spanish Revival motif. She designed residences (with characteristic redwood shingles), community buildings, and institutions that featured her trademark tasteful detailing, exposed sup-

Left: Julia Morgan as an architecture student in Paris. **Above:** The Neptune Pool of the Hearst Castle at San Simeon, designed by Morgan.

port beams, and beautifully functional form. But it was her rebuilding of the elegant Fairmont Hotel, which had been destroyed in the great earthquake of 1906, that firmly established her reputation and dramatically increased her demand. She designed YWCA facilities throughout California, and later Utah and Hawaii; Christian Science and Baptist churches; stores; university buildings; and estates.

When William Randolph Hearst selected Morgan to design San Simeon, she had been in practice for almost twenty years. With her engineering expertise, European training, and extensive use of reinforced concrete, Morgan was one of the few architects who was up to the enormity of the task. She oversaw every detail of the planning and construction of this unprecedented project, which included blending in sections of European castles and monasteries that had been purchased by Hearst. The resulting palace, both grand and grandiose, is still breathtaking. Over the next few decades, Hearst commissioned newspaper offices, vacation homes, and other buildings in what would eventually amount to one-third of Morgan's life work.

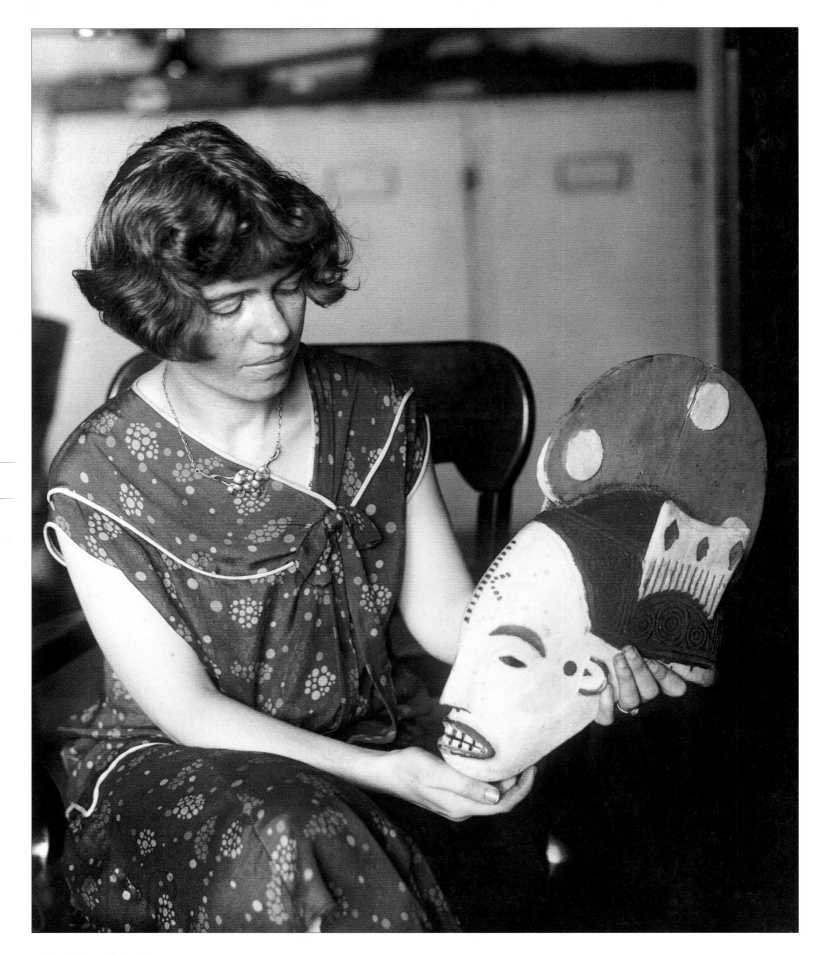

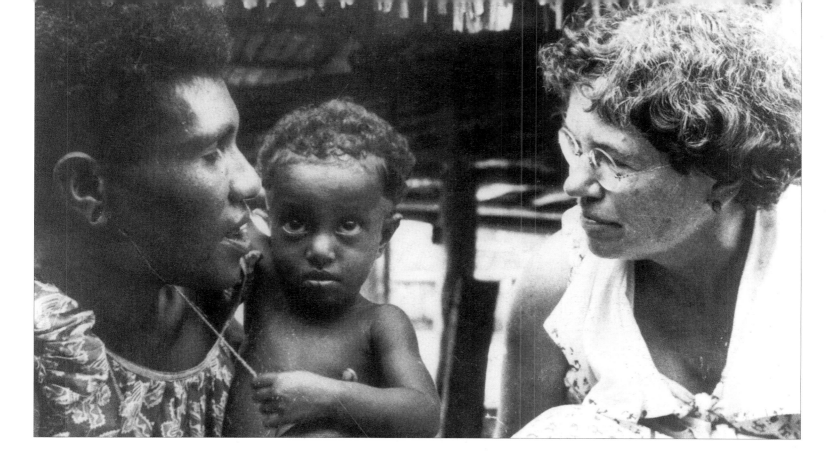

Above: Margaret Mead, who studied societies with little exposure to Western culture, with a Manus mother and child in the Admiralty Islands. **Opposite:** Mead holding a mask from the Bismark Archipelago in 1928.

Margaret Mead

anthropologist (1901–1978)

traight out of graduate school in 1925, Margaret Mead made the first of many trips to the South Seas, seeking to study human behavior in societies that had had the least exposure to Western culture. Having traveled halfway around the world to better understand her own homeland, Mead brought back startling insights, radical social critiques, and fresh ideas about American culture. Published in 1928, her enormously popular book *Coming of Age in Samoa* made cultural anthropology accessible to the public.

In contrasting the values of the two cultures—a method that would become her trademark—Mead challenged some of American society's rigid assumptions about gender, race, and sex. Mead focused her observations on the development of Samoan girls, who, like the boys, were raised by numerous adults in the community, enjoyed adolescence, and experimented sexually with members of both genders. She concluded that culture and environment had as strong an influence as biology on gender differences. Mead's subsequent field work in New Guinea and Bali also educated an ignorant American audience about the value and humanity of non-Western people. "We need every human gift and cannot afford to neglect any gift because of artificial barriers of sex or race or class or national origin," Mead wrote in 1949. "Instead of being presented with stereotypes by age, sex, color, class, or religion, children must have the opportunity to learn that within each range, some people are loathsome and some are delightful."

Mead's parents, an economics professor and a feminist sociologist, along with her paternal grandmother, strongly encouraged her adventuresome spirit and insatiable curiosity by schooling her at home in Philadelphia until the age of eleven. She later attended a one-room school, then earned her bachelor's degree from Barnard College and her master's and doctorate in anthropology from Columbia University.

She married sociologist Luther Cressman in 1923, two years before she left for Samoa. Mead did not change her name, however, telling her distraught father, "I am going to be famous some day, and I'm going to be known by my own name." A wise decision, as she soon divorced Cressman and married twice more. Mead's later work explored traditional male-female relationships, child-rearing practices, and the role of motherhood in perpetuating sex stereotypes. In 1939, the birth of her only child, Mary Catherine Bateson, shifted Mead's understanding and emphasis somewhat on the importance of maternity.

Mead enjoyed tremendous popularity, taught at Columbia University, and published nearly forty books and numerous articles. Still, she was strongly criticized for her research techniques—accused by her colleagues of not being thorough, not living long enough among her subjects, and not learning their languages. Mead maintained that her basic ideas were sound: that Americans could learn from people of other cultures, that embracing human sexuality (homosexual as well as heterosexual) is healthy, that women should be able to have societal roles besides motherhood, and that women are central to understanding any culture. Many of her insights and the presumptions they dispute continue to be vigorously debated today.

Amelia Earhart
aviator (1897–1937)

Amelia Earhart laid eyes on her first airplane on her tenth birthday at the Iowa State Fair. Although planes were quite a novelty, Earhart was unimpressed. "It was a thing of rusty wire and wood," she later wrote. But in 1920, she attended an air show in California and was captivated. "One thing I knew that day," she said, "I wanted to fly." Undeterred by the inherent danger and oblivious to the notion that it was all but unthinkable for a woman to pilot a plane, this charming daredevil from the Midwest went on to set an unmatched number of aviation records as she captured the heart and imagination of a nation.

Earhart arranged to take flying lessons from one of the first women aviators, Neta

Snook. Over the next several years, Earhart worked twenty-eight different jobs, from file clerk to truck driver, to support her flying. In 1922, she bought her first airplane, and in it she set the first of her many aviation records: highest altitude achieved by a woman pilot (14,000 feet, or 4,267.2m).

In 1928, Earhart was employed as a social worker in Boston when publisher and promoter George Putnam chose her to become the first woman to cross the Atlantic in an airplane—as a passenger. Even though the flight was genuinely risky, Earhart's presence was merely a publicity stunt. Nicknamed "Lady Lindy," after Charles Lindbergh, the first pilot to fly solo across the Atlantic, the charismatic Earhart became instantly famous when the plane landed safely in Wales. She was hailed as a hero and a role model for women, and she frequently spoke out on women's issues. But Earhart was unsatisfied, knowing that she had never taken the controls during the flight. "I wanted to make another flight alone," she later wrote. "I wanted to prove that I deserved at least a small fraction of the nice things said about me." So in 1932, Earhart piloted a Lockheed Vega from Newfoundland to

Below: Amelia Earhart (left) with other women aviators at a promotional event for their organization, The Ninety-Niners.
Opposite: Earhart with one of her planes.

Ireland, thus becoming the first woman to fly solo across the Atlantic.

Earhart completed two solo flights across the United States and set a multitude of distance, speed, and altitude records before deciding, at the age of thirty-nine, to do one last big flight. Her goal was the unprecedented feat of circumnavigating the globe at the equator. "I have a feeling that there is just about one more good flight left in my system," she remarked, "and I hope this trip is it."

On June 1, 1937, Earhart and navigator Fred Noonan set off from Miami, Florida, in a twin-engine Lockheed Electra. On July 2, as they were headed for tiny Howland Island in the South Pacific, trouble developed. Radio contact faltered, then failed altogether, and the plane disappeared. Despite extensive searches, no trace of Earhart, Noonan, or the plane was ever found. Over the years, Earhart's mysterious disappearance has fueled all kinds of rumor and speculation about what happened: Was she on a secret World War II reconnaissance mission for the U.S. government? Did she and Noonan survive and live out their days in the South Pacific? Regardless, what is known is that Amelia Earhart's heroic courage inspired generations of girls and women to reach for their dreams.

Charlayne Hunter–Gault
journalist (1942–)

When eighteen-year-old Charlayne Hunter arrived at the University of Georgia at Athens in 1961 to study journalism, she was greeted by jeers, threats, and burning crosses. One of the first two black students to attend the university, Hunter would sit in her dorm room at night and listen to mobs of white students yelling, "Two, four, six, eight, we don't want to integrate." Within a few days of her arrival, the chanting escalated to rioting. A brick came crashing through her window; the state police used tear gas to quell the disturbance; and she and the other black student, Hamilton Holmes, were temporarily removed from the campus.

Born in Due West, South Carolina, the oldest of three children, Charlayne moved with her family to Atlanta in 1951. She was educated in segregated schools with no blackboards, heat, or plumbing, and with hand-me-down books. "We didn't want to go to school with white people—that wasn't it," she later said. "It was those facilities they had." Inspired by the comic-strip character Brenda Starr, she wanted to be a journalist from the time she was a little girl, and she served as editor of her high school newspaper. The University of Georgia, the only college in the state with a journalism program, did not admit black students. Hunter and Holmes, with support of civil rights activists, applied for admission; their applications were denied. While lawyers fought it out in court, Hunter went to Wayne State University in Detroit. She and Holmes finally gained admission to the University of Georgia by court order. Twenty-five years after she graduated, Hunter-Gault returned to the university as its first black commencement speaker.

After college, Hunter started out as a secretary at *The New Yorker* magazine. A gifted writer, she contributed items to the column "The Talk of the Town" and before long was promoted to staff writer. In 1967, she moved to Washington, D.C., and

Below: Crowds gathered to watch Charlayne Hunter leave the registrar's office at the University of Georgia, where she became one of the first two black students to enroll.

Above: Top-notch journalist Hunter-Gault in 1978. **Right:**
Valentina Tereshkova, the first woman in space, in a triumphant
pose with Yuri Gagarin, the first man in space.

became a television anchorwoman and investigative reporter.
The following year she started a nine-year stint with *The New
York Times*, where she became the first Harlem bureau chief. In
1971, she married investment banker Ronald Gault.

In 1978, Hunter-Gault began her distinguished career as a
public television reporter when she joined the *MacNeil/Lehrer
NewsHour*. As the program's national correspondent, Hunter-
Gault won two Emmy awards for news and documentary reporting, and in 1986, she won a Peabody award for excellence in
broadcast journalism for her report on life in South Africa,
"Apartheid's People."

In 1996, Hunter-Gault moved with her husband to
Johannesburg to become the South Africa correspondent for
National Public Radio. She is known in the U.S. and internationally as a journalist of unquestionable integrity, and she brings to
her work the consciousness she developed as a civil rights pioneer. She says, "I have never apologized for doing black stories,
being interested in black stories, and insisting that every institution that I work for report black stories."

Valentina Tereshkova
cosmonaut (1937–)

*W*hen Valentina Tereshkova volunteered for the nascent
Soviet space program, the only thing she knew about
space flight was how to end it—she was an expert
parachutist. In the spring of 1962 she was one of five women
who entered the cosmonaut program at Star City in the Soviet
Union and underwent the same rigorous training as their male
colleagues, knowing that only one woman would be selected
for a historic mission. On June 16, 1963, in a rudimentary one-
person capsule called *Vostok 6*, Tereshkova was launched into
space and into the history books as the first woman to orbit the
earth. Almost twenty years would pass before another woman
traveled in space.

At the time, the Soviet Union and the United States were
engaged in an intricate game of one-upmanship; their playing
field was the unconquered heavens. The Soviets had already sent
two manned space flights up and back before an American astro-
naut got off the ground, but Soviet Premier Nikita Khrushchev
was looking for a public relations coup. He decided to send the

first woman into space, and further, that she would be an ordinary Russian factory worker or farmer.

Originally from central Russia, where she lived on a collective farm, Tereshkova moved with her family to Yaroslavl after her father was killed in World War II. At the age of sixteen, Tereshkova got a job as a spindler in a textile factory. In her spare time, she indulged in her love of parachuting and founded the Textile Mill Workers Parachute Club.

Like thousands of other Soviet men and women, Tereshkova wrote to the space program following the first successful manned flight into space by cosmonaut Yuri Gagarin in 1961. Explaining that Gagarin's triumphant flight was the most exciting day of her life, she described her extensive parachuting experience and her desire to become a cosmonaut. Much to her surprise, she was soon notified that she had been selected for the training program. With little more than one year before her flight, Tereshkova began to learn everything about rocket and spacecraft systems and to undergo intensive training in flying, weightlessness, isolation, and parachuting in a space suit.

The Soviets launched their space flights close together so that they could study the effects of space on two different people at the same time. Tereshkova's flight followed on the heels of *Vostok 5*, which took off two days earlier carrying male cosmonaut Valery Bykovsky. Tereshkova talked to Bykovsky by radio, saying, "It's beautiful up here. I can see the horizon. What beautiful colors." Together, the two cosmonauts sang songs to fall asleep.

Three days later, after orbiting the earth forty-eight times for a total distance of 1.2 million miles (1.93 million km), Tereshkova ejected herself from her capsule and safely parachuted down to Kazakhstan. She had remained in space longer than all of the U.S. Mercury astronauts combined. Tereshkova was named Hero of the Soviet Union, received numerous awards including the Order of Lenin, and brought great acclaim to her country on a world tour celebrating her achievement. She continued her aerospace career as an engineer and traveled extensively, lecturing on her flight and on women's issues. But Tereshkova will always be remembered for her brave journey, when she boldly went where no woman—and few men—had gone before.

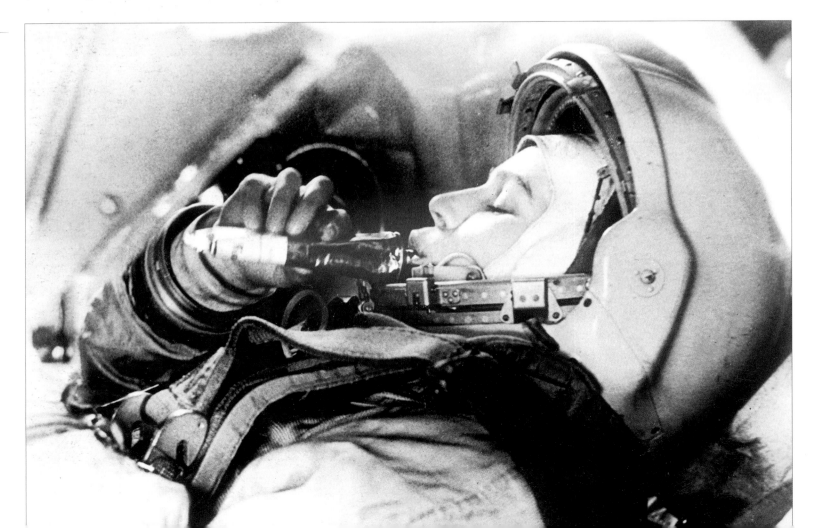

Twyla Tharp

choreographer and dancer (1941–)

*T*wyla Tharp's 1965 debut as a choreographer, in a solo dance piece she performed called *Tank Dive*, was as unconventional as the rest of her career: her performance lasted only four minutes. She had wanted to create one perfect dance; besides, Tharp reasoned, she didn't charge admission. Moving effortlessly among genres, Tharp's choreography—clever, playful, irreverent, original—turned the traditional dance world on its ear and continues to delight audiences around the world.

Tharp's early pieces featured dancers and non-dancers moving about public settings (like the central staircase at New York's Museum of Modern Art), generally without music, sets, or costumes. In the early 1970s, she incorporated jazz and created fuller, more popular dances. Tharp burst into the public's consciousness in 1973, with a delightful work called *Deuce Coupe*, which she created for her own troupe of seven dancers and the Joffrey Ballet, set to the music of the Beach Boys. Later that year, she produced *As Time Goes By* to music by Haydn for the Joffrey.

Having quickly earned a reputation as one of the most imaginative and popular choreographers in the world, Tharp was commissioned to create a piece for the American Ballet Theatre and its star, Mikhail Barishnikov. The intricate precision required by *Push Comes to Shove* (1976) was as technically demanding as the most difficult ballets that Barishnikov had danced, but Tharp also unleashed his considerable sense of humor. The popularity of *Push Comes to Shove* also brought out a few disgruntled critics; one called her "untutored" and described her style as "squiggly tic-and-twitchy." Tharp took this in stride. "There are so few people who can really take hold of art and sort of eat and chew it up," she said. "Somehow it's got to be held special, sacred in a corner, and if you don't do the same thing with it, if you're not equally reverential, serious, and pompous about it, well, then you're not a great artist. Who needs that?"

Below: Innovative choreographer Twyla Tharp relaxes after a dance rehearsal in 1993. **Opposite:** Tereshkova in her space suit during training for her 1963 flight.

45

Classically trained in music and dance, Tharp knows of what she rearranges. She was just two years old when she started taking piano lessons, and she later studied violin, viola, drums, music theory, and composition, as well as tap and ballet. When Tharp was ten, her family moved from her hometown of Portland, Indiana, to Los Angeles to run a chain of drive-in theaters. She moved to the East Coast to study with ballet teacher Igor Schwetzoff and trained in the New York studios of dance luminaries Martha Graham, Merce Cunningham, and Erick Hawkins, while earning a degree in art history from Barnard College. After performing with Paul Taylor's company for a year, Tharp founded her own troupe.

In addition to many live works, Tharp choreographed the films *Hair*, *Ragtime*, *Amadeus*, and *White Knights*. In 1988, she disbanded her company and joined the American Ballet Theatre as an artistic associate. She published her autobiography, *Push Comes to Shove*, in 1992. With an air of nonchalance, wit, and easy grace that belies the complexity of her work, Tharp remains one of the most innovative talents in dance in modern times.

Shirley Chisholm
politician (1924–)

As a student at Brooklyn College in the 1940s, Shirley Chisholm became furious when a local white politician told a college audience, "Black people will advance someday, but black people are always going to need to have white people leading them." She made up her mind to challenge his assumption personally and built an impressive career in public service and politics, even running for the presidency of the United States.

Chisholm's parents were originally from Barbados, and during the Depression, poverty forced them to send their Brooklyn-born daughters back to the island to stay with family. Chisholm loved those six years on the farm where she lived with her grandmother, a woman who taught her "pride, courage, and faith."

After earning a graduate degree in elementary education from Columbia University in 1952, Chisholm ran a Manhattan child care center and later became a consultant to the City of New York on child welfare issues. In 1964, she was elected to the New York state legislature, where she promoted children's rights. Her outspoken, straightforward style, grassroots experience, and fluency in Spanish appealed to the people of her district, who were predominantly black and Puerto Rican. Four years later, using the slogan "Unbought and Unbossed," she was elected to represent them in Congress.

Chisholm was the first African-American woman elected to the U.S. House of Representatives, where she served for fourteen years. A zealous advocate for civil rights and women's rights, she championed welfare reform, education, employment, health care, housing, job training, the Equal Rights Amendment, and repro-

Below: Shirley Chisholm flashes a "V" for victory after becoming the first black woman elected to Congress.

ductive freedom. "Laws will not eliminate prejudice from the hearts of human beings," she said on the floor of the House in 1970. "But that is no reason to allow prejudice to continue to be enshrined in our laws to perpetuate injustice through inaction."

In 1972, Chisholm made an unprecedented bid for the presidency. Acknowledging from the start that she couldn't win (she was drastically underfunded and largely ignored by the media and her opponents), Chisholm nonetheless was deadly serious about campaigning—hoping to open people's eyes to the possibility that "someday, somewhere, somehow, someone other than a white male could be president." While her campaign mobilized students, grassroots feminists, and urban community groups, national feminist and civil rights organizations were publicly cautious. Although she was a member of the National Organization for Women, a founder of the National Women's Political Caucus, and a spokesperson for the National Abortion

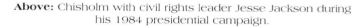

Above: Chisholm with civil rights leader Jesse Jackson during his 1984 presidential campaign.

Rights Action League, most national women's organizations gave their early support to George McGovern. Even more painful for Chisholm was the public attitude of prominent black male leaders, who let it be known that the first black person to run for the presidency should be male. (Only the Black Panthers officially endorsed her candidacy.) "I have met with far more discrimination as a woman than being black in the field of politics," she said. Still, she captured more than 150 votes on the first ballot at the Democratic convention.

Chisholm served in Congress until 1982, when she retired from public office. Not one to rest on her laurels, she continues to advocate her progressive agenda through teaching and lecturing—true to her maxim that "service is the rent that you pay for room on this earth."

Geraldine Ferraro

politician (1935–)

When Geraldine Ferraro stepped on stage to accept the Democratic nomination for vice president of the United States, she thought she was seeing things. Amid the pandemonium, she scanned the sea of screaming, cheering, crying faces; she thought she saw women everywhere she looked. In fact, many male delegates had turned over their floor passes so that female alternates could bear witness as Ferraro made history. "My name is Geraldine Ferraro," she began, "and I stand here before you to proclaim tonight: America is the land where dreams can come true for all of us." On July 19, 1984, this tough, smart daughter of Italian immigrants became the first woman selected by a major party to run for the office of vice president.

For the next four months, she traveled throughout the country, bringing a message of hope and possibility to electrified, record-breaking crowds of women and men. The campaign trail was at times brutal, with journalists, politicians, and funders grilling Ferraro relentlessly on everything from whether she would be able to "push the button" and fire nuclear weapons, to what she would wear for the vice presidential debate. "It was so endlessly annoying to be presumed as weak and indecisive because I was a woman," she later wrote in her book, *Ferraro: My Story*.

At a critical point in the campaign, Ferraro faced hundreds of reporters at an unprecedented press conference to answer allegations about her family's finances and her husband's alleged involvement in improper real estate transactions. Ferraro answered every question with her characteristic candor and tenacity, passing another crucial test of nerve with flying colors. However, the historic Walter Mondale/Geraldine Ferraro ticket lost to Ronald Reagan and George Bush that November.

Ferraro had developed her resilience as a young girl. Her father died suddenly when she was eight years old, leaving the family with little money. Her mother, Antonetta, supported her children by crocheting beads onto dresses. She was determined that her daughter would get an education, and Ferraro attended Marymount College in New York on a scholarship. In 1960, after earning a law degree at night while teaching English in New York City public schools during the day, Ferraro married John Zaccaro and spent more than a decade at home raising three children. Returning to the paid workforce, she created the Special Victims Bureau at the district attorney's office, where she oversaw the prosecution of sex crimes, child abuse, domestic violence, and violent crimes against the elderly. Elected to Congress in 1978, Ferraro was, during her three terms, a vocal opponent of the Reagan Administration's economic policies and a fierce advocate for the rights of women and older people.

Whenever Geraldine Ferraro faced her toughest moments, she remembered what her mother would tell her when she was young. "Don't forget your name," Antonetta would say. "*Ferro* means iron. You can bend it, but you can't break it. Go on."

Below: Geraldine Ferraro makes an impressive showing in her debate with Vice President George Bush. **Opposite:** Ferraro's vice presidential candidacy ignited a new sense of possibility in American women.

her journal with frostbitten fingers. Bancroft and five men reached the North Pole on May 1, 1986.

Back home in St. Paul, Minnesota, Bancroft found herself in great demand for media interviews and appearances. Terrified of public speaking, she yearned to get back to the solitude of the wilderness. Over the next few years, she designed the American Women's Expedition (AWE) to Antarctica—the coldest, windiest, driest place in the world. Bancroft had publicly identified herself as a lesbian in 1988, and she frequently encountered homophobia and sexism as she pulled together her expedition. Denied the corporate sponsorship that usually supports such treks, Bancroft and her team of three other world-class athletes set out for Antarctica with frayed cold-weather gear and secondhand equipment.

For sixty-seven days, Bancroft and her teammates skied directly into the bitter Antarctic wind, pulling 200-pound (90.8kg) sleds loaded with supplies for eight to fourteen hours per day. "The goal was not so much reaching the Pole itself," Bancroft mused. "It was a bit more universal. Why do we take on struggles? Why run a marathon? I think we're all striving to push ourselves, and in the process of overcoming struggles and challenges, we get to know ourselves better." Overcoming 660 miles (1061.9km) of treacherous crevasses and massive ice drifts, the women reached the South Pole on January 14, 1993. Bancroft is the only woman in history to trek to both Poles.

Bancroft was always an adventurer, climbing out of her crib even before she could walk. Despite a severe learning disability, she was determined to become a teacher. She taught physical and special education in the Minnesota public schools before quitting to train for the North Pole trip.

Bancroft also works as an expedition leader for Wilderness Inquiry, a program that takes people of all skill levels and physical abilities on wilderness treks around the world. People with disabilities discover untapped strengths, and able-bodied people dismantle their preconceived notions about ability and courage. "I think the things we overcome in life really become our strengths," said Bancroft. "Those are our pressure ridges of ice.... I used all my strengths and all my weaknesses to get me to the top of the world."

Above: Ann Bancroft reaches the treacherous summit of Mt. McKinley, one of her early conquests.

Ann Bancroft
polar explorer (1955–)

As the sole woman on the 1986 Steger Expedition to the North Pole, Ann Bancroft fended off wolves, pulled herself out of the frigid black waters of the Arctic Ocean, and drove a dogsled hundreds of miles in temperatures with a windchill hovering around one hundred degrees below zero. "I had fun," she later said with characteristic simplicity. After becoming the first woman in history to trek to the North Pole, the charismatic Bancroft led her own all-women expedition to the other end of the earth—Antarctica.

Bancroft thrived on the daily challenge of forging a trail to the North Pole, chopping through ice and pressure ridges that ran up to forty feet (12.2m) high. As the only woman on the trip, she kept to herself. At night, she would unfreeze the ink in her pen by placing it in her armpit, and write her thoughts in

50

Cynthia Cooper
athlete (1963–)

On August 30, 1997, Cynthia Cooper stood with her teammates before a crowd of 16,285 delirious fans at the Houston Summit arena and savored the moment. She had just led the Houston Comets to the first-ever Women's National Basketball Association (WNBA) championship. For the thirty-four-year-old Cooper, the league's leading scorer and most valuable player, the victory was all the sweeter because of her years of paying dues on and off the court.

The woman who took the new league by storm and secured a permanent place in basketball history didn't even start playing until she was sixteen. Born in Chicago, the fifth of eight children, Cooper was raised in the impoverished Watts section of Los Angeles by her mother, Mary Cobbs. In high school, she was a track star and also played softball, volleyball, and badminton. But even with her late start in basketball, she won a scholarship to the University of Southern California, where she played a supporting role to hoop stars Cheryl Miller and twins Pamela and Paula McGee on the championship teams of 1983 and 1984. "I was always the sort of player who was asked to pass the ball to the marquee players and set picks, run the fast break," she later said. "But all along, I told myself...this is not all I can do."

When Cooper graduated, there were no professional opportunities in the U.S., so, like many outstanding American women basketball players, she moved to Europe, playing in Spain and Italy for eleven years. A member of the medal-winning 1988 and 1992 U.S. Olympic teams, and her league's leading scorer eight times, she dreamed of coming home.

In January of 1997, her dream came true when she signed with the Houston Comets. But just weeks later, her mother was diagnosed with breast cancer. During the season, even as she was averaging 22.2 points per game and setting league scoring records of thirty, thirty-two, and finally forty-four points in a game, Cooper was overseeing her mother's care, shuttling her to doctors' offices for tests or chemotherapy treatments. She is also helping to raise two nephews and a niece. Sustaining her are her strong Christian faith and her devotion to her mom. One of

Cooper's proudest achievements was winning the gold medal as part of the 1988 U.S. Olympic team and presenting it to her mother on September 29, her mother's birthday.

Cooper, affectionately known as "Coop," electrified audiences with her unstoppable athleticism, gesturing to the fans to "raise the roof" when the Comets got a basket. Her astonishing skill and irrepressible spirit drew thousands of new fans to the game and swept her team to the top. The WNBA's inaugural season was a victory for women's sports and a personal triumph for league MVP Cynthia Cooper.

Below: League MVP Cynthia Cooper's athleticism dazzled the fans during the Women's National Basketball Association's inaugural season.

COURAGE OF HER CONVICTIONS

Ida B. Wells-Barnett, journalist

Jeannette Rankin, peace activist and politician

Rosa Parks, civil rights activist

Dolores Fernández Huerta, labor leader

Fannie Lou Hamer, civil rights activist

Marian Wright Edelman, children's advocate

Helen Caldicott, peace activist

Faye Wattleton, reproductive rights activist

Wilma Mankiller, chief

Chai Ling, revolutionary

Aung San Suu Kyi, political leader

―――――∞∞∞――――――

In the face of resistance, public ridicule, or even mortal danger, these women listened to their hearts and trusted their unshakable faith. In standing up for what they believed in, they spoke out for the many who dared not.

Fannie Lou Hamer

Jeannette Rankin

Helen Caldicott

Aung San Suu Kyi

Rosa Parks

Chai Ling

Faye Wattleton

Marian Wright Edelman

Ida B. Wells-Barnett

Ida B. Wells-Barnett
journalist (1862–1931)

Sharp-tongued and harshly opinionated, Ida B. Wells-Barnett had many political enemies and few close friends, but she was one of the most influential journalists and black leaders of her time. Born into slavery in Mississippi, Wells-Barnett preached that agitation, activism, and economic independence were the keys to self-actualization for African Americans, and led by example. Her lifelong anti-lynching crusade put her life in danger, but her exposés nearly put an end to these brutal killings.

After her parents and youngest brother died in a yellow fever epidemic, sixteen-year-old

Ida was determined to keep her five remaining siblings together. Her mother's family had been torn apart through slavery, and in her honor, young Ida vowed to raise her brothers and sisters herself. She took a teaching position and cared for her family, eventually with help from relatives like her Aunt Fannie, who invited Ida and her sisters to live with her in Memphis.

Wells flourished in the big city, attending plays and lectures, participating in public readings, teaching school in nearby Woodstock, and soon becoming editor of *Evening Star*, a black literary journal. Writing passionately in plain language about issues that concerned African Americans, she created articles that were picked up in black weeklies throughout the country. She joined the staff of the weekly *Free Speech and Headlight* in Memphis on the condition that she could purchase a one-third ownership in the paper. Wells soon increased the circulation of the paper enough to quit teaching and concentrate on writing.

In 1892, the lynching of her friend Thomas Moss and his two business partners irrevocably changed her life. While most lynchings were alleged to be punishment for rape of white women by black men, Wells saw that the motive was often economic—Moss's grocery store, for example, drew business from his white competitors. Wells threw herself into documenting the circumstances that had led to more than seven hundred lynchings over the previous decade. When Wells's inflammatory editorial was published—asserting that rape charges factored into only one-third of the cases, that white men raped black women with impunity, and that white resentment of blacks' economic autonomy fueled the rape charges—she was en route to New York for a speaking engagement. Upon arrival, she learned that the *Free Speech* office had been burned to the ground and whites were calling for her lynching. Wells would not return to Memphis for thirty years, continuing her activism in New York and Chicago. Nor did she soften her approach, writing, "Having lost my paper, had a price put on my life, and been made an exile from home for hinting at the truth, I felt that I owed it to myself and my race to

Above: Congresswoman Jeannette Rankin is presented with the flag flown over the House of Representatives during the passage of the suffrage amendment in 1918. **Opposite:** Ida B. Wells-Barnett risked her life to put an end to lynching.

tell the whole truth now that I was where I could do so freely." She married Chicago publisher Ferdinand Barnett in 1895 and continued her civil rights work while raising their four children. Wells-Barnett left no stone unturned in her quest for justice for African Americans. "There must always be a remedy for wrong and injustice if we only know how to find it," she wrote.

Jeannette Rankin
peace activist and politician (1880–1973)

our days after she took office as the first woman elected to the U.S. House of Representatives, Jeannette Rankin was faced with a momentous vote: should the United States declare war on Germany and thus enter World War I? "I want to stand by my country, but I cannot vote for war," she said simply. "I vote no." Some twenty-four years later, on the day

after the Japanese attack on Pearl Harbor, the newly re-elected congresswoman faced another fateful decision. This time, Rankin cast the sole vote against U.S. entry into World War II.

In both cases, her vote cost Rankin her seat in Congress— she served only two terms in her lifetime. In both cases, she had no regrets. "It was not only the most significant thing *I* ever did," she said of her 1917 vote. "It was a significant thing in itself."

The oldest of seven children in a ranching family outside Missoula, Montana, Rankin graduated from the University of Montana in 1902. After a brief stint as a social worker, she moved to Seattle, Washington, and was swept up in the state campaign for women's suffrage. (At this time, the suffrage movement had adopted mainly a state-by-state strategy.)

By 1911, she was back home, lobbying the Montana state legislature for women's right to vote. Over the next few years she worked for suffrage in another fifteen states, eventually becoming the legislative secretary of the National American Woman Suffrage Association. In that capacity, Rankin finally helped win women's suffrage in Montana in 1914.

COURAGE OF HER CONVICTIONS

Two years later, Rankin mobilized her state's newly enfranchised women and their progressive male allies to elect her as the first woman in the U.S. House of Representatives—four years before women had the right to vote nationally. In Congress, she was a progressive voice, a vocal advocate for equal opportunity for women, aid to children, freedom of speech, and, of course, a federal women's suffrage amendment.

Rankin's explanation for her initial antiwar position that she felt that her constituents didn't support the war. Over time, though, she developed a sophisticated pacifist philosophy, which she effectively communicated to the public in simple terms. Throughout the 1920s and 1930s, Rankin worked for a number of antiwar groups, including the Women's Peace Union (whose goal was a constitutional amendment to outlaw war), the National Council for the Prevention of War, and the Women's International League for Peace and Freedom.

In 1940, as war raged in Europe, Rankin was again elected to Congress. Although she had run as a pacifist, her vote against the declaration of war infuriated the public and eliminated any chance of re-election.

After leaving office, Rankin became a rancher in Montana and traveled around the world to learn more about pacifist philosophies. She was particularly captured by the work of Mohandas Gandhi and made seven trips to India between 1946 and 1971. She remained steadfastly opposed to U.S. military interventions, including in Korea and Vietnam. On January 15, 1968, she led a band of five thousand protesters, dubbed the Jeannette Rankin Brigade, on a march on the Capitol to protest the Vietnam War. She was eighty-seven years old.

To the end, she shared her clear vision of the hope of peace and the futility of war, with her message that "You can no more win a war than you can win an earthquake."

Above: Rosa Parks is joined by the Rev. Martin Luther King Jr. in 1965 at a Southern Christian Leadership Council dinner in her honor. **Opposite:** Jeannette Rankin in 1917.

Rosa Parks
civil rights activist (1913–)

t is an unforgettable moment in the history of the United States. On December 1, 1955, Rosa Parks, a seamstress and the secretary of the Montgomery, Alabama, chapter of the National Association for the Advancement of Colored People (NAACP), defied local law, Southern custom, and generations of racism by refusing to give up her seat on a bus to a white man. With that single, courageous act, Parks sparked the 381-day Montgomery bus boycott—the crystallizing event for the emerging civil rights movement.

At the time, the law dictated that black people had to step onto the bus through the front door to pay the fare, then get off the bus and re-enter through the back door to sit down. When

COURAGE OF HER CONVICTIONS

the front section was full, black people were expected to stand so that white people could sit.

One of the myths about Rosa Parks is that she was just tired that day. "When I left the store that evening I was tired," she said, "but I was tired every day." Although her refusal was unplanned, Parks had been active for years in civil rights work. Both she and her husband, Raymond, were longtime members of the NAACP and part of a group of activists who wanted to challenge the discriminatory practices of the Montgomery bus company. The previous summer, Parks had attended a training session for activists and organizers at the Highlander Folk School in Monteagle, Tennessee.

For refusing to give up her seat, Parks was arrested and charged under the local segregation ordinance. NAACP officials and other activists sprung into action, calling for a boycott of the bus company and challenging the discriminatory law in federal court. They formed the Montgomery Improvement Association and elected as their president a twenty-six-year-old pastor named Martin Luther King Jr.

Throughout the yearlong boycott, thousands of ordinary bus riders walked up to twelve miles (19km) a day, carpooled, or sacrificed getting to where they wanted to go. The boycott virtually crippled the bus company, since three-quarters of its ridership was black. On November 13, 1956, the Supreme Court ruled the segregation laws unconstitutional.

The personal costs of Parks's act of courage were high: Raymond left his job as a barber after his boss forbade any discussion in his shop of Rosa or the boycott. When Parks lost her job, she was unable able to find work in Montgomery. In 1957, the couple moved to Detroit, where Parks was eventually hired by Representative John Conyers as a staff assistant, a position she held until her retirement in 1988.

In 1987, she founded the Rosa and Raymond Parks Institute of Self-Development, which offers young people classes, scholarships, career training, and the opportunity to learn about the heritage of the civil rights movement.

"As I recall the history of racism over the past generations, it brings back memories I would rather forget," reflected Parks in her 1995 book *Quiet Strength*. "But since I cannot forget them, I try to use them to bring about change. By traveling the country and talking about civil rights history, I am not living in the past. I am fighting for more justice. I will keep struggling for freedom and equality as long as I have the strength."

Dolores Fernández Huerta
labor leader (1930–)

Shortly after Dolores Fernández began teaching in the 1950s, she became frustrated with the limits of the profession. "I realized one day that as a teacher I couldn't do anything for the kids who came to school barefoot and hungry," she said. She quit her job to organize for social justice in California's Mexican-American community. As co-founder and first vice president of the United Farm Workers (UFW) union, she has devoted more than thirty-five years to improving the working conditions and lives of predominantly Mexican migrant workers and their families.

Below: UFW leader Dolores Huerta passionately advocates for a national boycott of grapes, 1988. **Opposite:** Rosa Parks sits in the front of a Montgomery, Alabama, city bus in 1956 as a Supreme Court ruling banning segregation on the city's public transportation takes effect.

Huerta (who changed her name when she married her second husband, Ventura Huerta, in the mid-1950s) and co-founder Cesar Chavez met in the late 1950s while working for the Community Service Organization (CSO), a Mexican-American self-help group. Huerta's forceful style and passionate advocacy had landed her the position of lobbyist to the state legislature, where she focused on the plight of migrant workers, who were unprotected by any union.

In 1962, Huerta and Chavez formed the Farm Workers Association, later renamed the United Farm Workers. From its inception, the union's vision was clear and the challenge colossal. "We want to change people's lives," said Huerta. "Farmworkers kill themselves working, living nowhere, traveling all the time, putting up with pesticides because the growers want it that way.... We know the work can be organized so people settle down in one place with their families, and control their lives through political power and their own union—which they run themselves."

Huerta quickly proved herself an effective strategist and leader, organizing local strikes that led to improved working conditions for farm workers. Although she had never read a contract before she first sat down at the bargaining table, she became the union's most effective negotiator. In the 1970s, undaunted by her constituents' lack of economic and political strength, she mobilized a coalition of Hispanic organizations, unions, students, activists, peace groups, religious groups, feminists, and concerned consumers to support her cause through national grape, lettuce, and Gallo wine boycotts. The combined economic pressure forced the passage of the Agriculture Labor Relations Act in 1975, the first law to recognize the collective bargaining rights of farm workers in California.

Throughout Huerta's years of organizing, she raised her eleven children—two from a brief marriage to her high school sweetheart, five with her second husband, and four with her longtime companion, Richard Chavez (Cesar's brother)—with significant help from her mother, her friends, and the union community.

Arrested more than twenty times throughout her life, Huerta was viciously attacked by San Francisco police in 1988 at a peaceful demonstration protesting the policies of George Bush. Clubbed repeatedly, she suffered six broken ribs and underwent emergency surgery to have her spleen removed. The public outcry about her assault led to a change in police department rules for crowd control and police discipline. After an extensive recovery period and a record settlement, Huerta gradually returned to work at the UFW. In recent years, she took a leave from the union to help elect Mexican-American women candidates to the California state legislature.

"I think we brought to the world, the United States anyway, the whole idea of boycotting as a nonviolent tactic," said Huerta. "I think we have laid a pattern of how farm workers are eventually going to get out of their bondage. It may not happen right now in our foreseeable future, but the pattern is there and farm workers are going to make it."

Fannie Lou Hamer
civil rights activist (1917–1977)

"I 'm sick and tired of being sick and tired" was the rallying cry of Fannie Lou Hamer, an irrepressible spirit who fought for basic human rights for the most disenfranchised Americans.

The youngest of twenty children born to dirt-poor sharecroppers in Ruleville, Mississippi, Fannie Lou Townsend started working in the cotton fields at the age of six. She married Perry "Pap" Hamer, and together they were sharecroppers for eighteen years on a nearby farm. In 1962, when workers for the Student Nonviolent Coordinating Committee (SNCC) came to town looking for volunteers to challenge the exclusion of black people from the voter rolls, Hamer signed up immediately. For attempting to register to vote, Hamer was fired and her family was kicked off the farm.

In 1963, Hamer became a registered voter and a field secretary for SNCC, marking the beginning of a lifetime crusade for social justice. Noted for her down-to-earth personal style, her uncompromising political stances, her rousing oratory, and her disarming sense of humor, Hamer eloquently represented the concerns of the least powerful. She paid a steep price; she was

shot at, firebombed, and harassed, and while jailed in 1963 for attempting to register blacks to vote, Hamer was badly beaten and never fully recovered from her injuries.

It would take more to keep Hamer down, however. Soon after registering to vote, she ran for Congress and lost. Unfazed, she and two other black women went to Congress and lobbied lawmakers to disallow the results of the election because blacks had been excluded. The House voted against their proposal, 228-143. Hamer pressed on.

One of Hamer's most brazen acts came in 1964, at the Democratic National Convention in Atlantic City, New Jersey. She and other members of the Mississippi Freedom Democratic Party were at the convention to challenge the seating of the all-white delegation from Mississippi. Hamer gave a dramatic, nationally televised speech to the credentials committee describing the violence and intimidation used by the state party to keep black people out, including the jailhouse beating she had

suffered. "All of this on account we want to register, to become first-class citizens," she told the committee, "and if the Freedom Democratic Party is not seated now, I question America—is this America, the land of the free and the home of the brave, where we have to sleep with our telephones off the hooks because our lives be threatened daily because we want to live as decent human beings, in America?"

Hamer and her colleagues weren't seated, but the national party resolved to no longer recognize any delegations that were not integrated. Hamer herself was part of the Mississippi delegation to the 1968 convention.

Aware of the connection between racism and poverty and political exclusion, Hamer worked hard not just for the rights of black people but for the empowerment of poor people. She once told a reporter, "With the people, for the people, by the people—I crack up when I hear it; I say, with the handful, for the handful, by the handful, 'cause that's really what happens."

Hamer drew her deepest strength from her profound Christian faith. Her trademark song, "This Little Light of Mine," will forever be associated with the hope and determination she embodied.

61

Marian Wright Edelman
children's advocate (1939–)

*A*s far back as she can remember, Marian Wright Edelman's parents instilled in her a respect for community service. "Service was as much a part of my upbringing as eating breakfast and going to school," she said. "It isn't something that you do in your spare time. It was clear that it was the very purpose of life." She took their message to heart. As founder and president of the Children's Defense Fund (CDF), Edelman has been a relentless and compelling advocate for the health, safety, and welfare of children and their families.

After graduating from Spelman College in Atlanta in 1960, she had hoped to pursue an advanced degree in Russian studies, but the growing intensity of the U.S. civil rights struggle persuaded her to become a lawyer instead. She attended Yale Law School and in 1964 became the first African-American woman to pass the Bar in the state of Mississippi, where—although she was on several occasions threatened and jailed—she registered black voters, defended civil rights activists, lobbied for Head Start funding, and directed the NAACP Legal Defense and Educational Fund in Jackson. In 1973, she settled in Washington, D.C., and started CDF, the nation's most effective voice for the rights of children.

Appalled at the country's lack of concern and funding for children, the fast-talking, energetic Edelman has tirelessly pressed Congress and the public to invest time and money in the next generation. "It is a spiritually impoverished nation that permits infants and children to be the poorest Americans," she wrote in 1992. "If we do not act immediately to protect America's children and change the misguided national choices that leave too many of them unhealthy, unhoused, ill-fed and undereducated, the consequences will be frightening."

CDF lobbies for increased spending on prenatal and infant health care, quality child care, education, and family support systems; it pays particular attention to the needs of poor, minority, and disabled children. CDF also produces memorable public service campaigns, like the teen pregnancy prevention ads that featured a high school football player holding a newborn with the tag line, "An extra seven pounds could keep you off the football team," or a teenage girl holding an infant in her lap under the headline, "It's like being grounded for eighteen years."

Since she is well known as the preeminent children's crusader, Edelman's passionate opinions appear frequently in interviews and editorial pieces, as well as in her popular books, which include *Families in Peril: An Agenda for Social Change* (1987) and *The Measure of Our Success: A Letter to My Children and Yours* (1992). On June 1, 1996, Edelman convened the Stand for Children rally in Washington, D.C., in which throngs of Americans from all fifty states gathered to demonstrate their concern for the well-being of the country's children. Edelman calls Stand for Children, now an annual event in hundreds of cities nationwide, "a triumph of spirit and commitment to our children."

Although she has said, "I feel like I've been doing it forever," Edelman's personal commitment to children is unwavering: "The legacy I want to leave is a child care system that says that no kid is going to be left alone or unsafe."

Below: Marian Wright Edelman, the feisty founder of the Children's Defense Fund, lobbies relentlessly for the rights of children.

Helen Caldicott
peace activist (1938–)

*A*s a teenager in Melbourne, Australia, Helen Caldicott read Nevil Shute's *On the Beach*, a terrifying novel set in her hometown in which the human race is annihilated by nuclear war. Caldicott never forgot the chilling story, and years later, as she watched the international arms race escalate, she was determined to prevent fiction from becoming a reality. The world's most compelling and well-known champion of nuclear disarmament, for almost three decades Caldicott has been arguing persuasively that the abolition of nuclear weapons is, for each of us, a matter of life and death.

As a pediatrician specializing in cystic fibrosis, Caldicott saw many of her young patients die. She knew that the incidence of cystic fibrosis, as well as leukemia and other cancers, would increase as the radiation in the environment increased, and she decided that "promoting the elimination of nuclear weapons and power was part of practicing pediatrics and real preventive medicine." In 1971, Caldicott earned a national reputation by leading a demonstration to stop nuclear bomb tests by the French government in the South Pacific, which had produced high levels of radioactivity in southern Australia's drinking water.

Six years later, when she relocated to Boston with her husband and three children, she founded Physicians for Social Responsibility (PSR), a group of physicians who educated their colleagues about the dangers of nuclear power, nuclear weapons, and nuclear war. Uncanny timing pushed the nascent group into the limelight. They placed an ad in the *New England Journal of Medicine*; the day before it appeared, the infamous accident at the Three Mile Island nuclear power plant in Harrisburg, Pennsylvania, occurred. Caldicott addressed a nervous crowd in Harrisburg a few weeks later, using her gift of making the scientific and medical consequences understandable through plain, graphic language. "Imagine: if one pound of plutonium were crushed in bits, and a bit were placed in the lungs of every person on the earth, it would kill us all," she told them. "One pound. And yet a one-thousand-megawatt nuclear plant produces roughly five hundred pounds of it a year."

Above: At a 1983 press conference in Boston, Dr. Helen Caldicott speaks out forcefully against the deployment of nuclear weapons in Europe.

Soon Caldicott was traveling constantly, giving lectures, speaking at conferences and rallies, and meeting with world leaders. "Sometimes I have so much to say and so little time that everything I say sounds jumbled to me," she lamented. Outspoken and charismatic, she tailored her speech to her audience—women would hear about the faces of burned children, men would hear about the effects of radiation on testicles. Few who heard her were unmoved. Obsessed with her mission to abolish nuclear weapons, in 1980 she gave up her medical practice to head up PSR full time. By 1983, up to eighty percent of the public supported some form of disarmament. In 1985, PSR's umbrella organization, the International Physicians for the Prevention of Nuclear War, received the Nobel Peace Prize.

At home, Caldicott tries to relax. "I can't live with the fears and worry all the time," she said. "I concentrate on the beauty of music, my flowers, my children."

Faye Wattleton
reproductive rights activist (1943–)

*L*ike her fundamentalist preacher mother, Faye Wattleton is charismatic, committed, passionate, and clear about her mission. But instead of traveling around to churches and revivals saving souls, Wattleton's crusade has been preaching about the righteousness of reproductive freedom. During her fourteen years as president of Planned Parenthood Federation of America, Wattleton was an imposing, steadfast, and savvy leader.

At the time she took the helm, just five years after the Supreme Court ruled that abortion was constitutionally protected, reproductive rights were under intensifying attack. Planned Parenthood clinics and other women's health facilities were being bombed, and their personnel threatened. Abortion rights were being eroded legally. Wattleton responded by transforming Planned Parenthood—which had been known primarily for its family planning services—into an aggressive, visible lobby.

Wattleton spoke to audiences around the country, testified before Congress, and appeared on television debates. Her message was clear, consistent, and basic: "Women can't control their lives unless they can control their fertility." As a result, she started to get death threats and had to travel with bodyguards.

After graduating from high school in St. Louis, Missouri, at age sixteen, Wattleton studied nursing at Ohio State University and earned a master's degree in maternal and infant health care from Columbia University. During an internship at Harlem Hospital in 1966 and, later, working for the Public Health Department in Dayton, Ohio, Wattleton witnessed firsthand the consequences of illegal abortion—terrified young mothers; teenagers whose bodies were too immature to sustain a pregnancy; women dead or seriously injured from abortions using bleach or Lysol or knitting needles or coat hangers or sticks.

Memories of these women stayed with her and fueled her insistence that abortion is a necessary right for women. "Women will always, and have always, controlled their fertility," she later said, "and they won't stop even if pro-criminalist forces have their way. They will simply once again face injury and death in their determination not to bear unwanted children."

She volunteered for Planned Parenthood and, in 1970, became executive director of the Miami Valley, Ohio, affiliate. In 1978, at the age of 34, Wattleton became president of Planned Parenthood Federation of America, the nation's oldest and largest family planning organization, with hundreds of affiliates providing medical services to nearly four million people a year.

Below: Pro-choice firebrand Faye Wattleton (right, with colleague Kate Michelman) testifies before the Senate Judiciary Committee in 1990.

Wattleton's mother once told her that the year Wattleton started working for Planned Parenthood "was a year that I will never forget. I lost my husband and I lost my daughter." Ozie Wattleton had publicly requested prayers for her daughter's salvation. Yet Wattleton still feels a strong connection to her mother and even sees parallels in the passion each brings to her work: "I am my mother's daughter, and very proud to be so," she once said. "I came from a mother who did what she wanted to do.... Her calling was her choice. Her unflinching opposition to sin was like my unflinching opposition to intolerance."

Wilma Mankiller
chief (1945–)

I n July of 1987, Wilma Mankiller was elected by a landslide to the highest office in her land—principal chief of the Cherokee Nation. The first woman in history to serve as chief of a major Native American tribe, Mankiller created a network of rural health care centers that became a model for the country, launched community development projects, and strengthened the preservation of Cherokee culture and language. Under Mankiller's leadership, the Cherokee economic base greatly improved and its dependence on the federal government diminished. "For me, the rewards came from attempting to break the cycle of poverty," she later wrote.

She was raised with her ten siblings on Mankiller Flats, Oklahoma, a 160-acre (64ha) tract of land deeded to her grandfather by the federal government. (The title Mankiller denotes a high Cherokee military rank; one of her ancestors adopted it as the family name.) Living by subsistence farming, the Mankillers had no running water or electricity. The farm failed when Wilma was eleven years old after a two-year drought. In a terrifying shift, her entire family was relocated overnight to an urban ghetto in San Francisco through a federal program of the U.S. government.

Becoming a progressive activist, Mankiller spent years organizing and working for Indian civil and treaty rights in San Francisco. Returning home to Mankiller Flats in 1977, she created and managed community renewal projects. After surviving a

65

near-fatal car accident in 1979 and several bouts with a life-threatening kidney disease, Mankiller had a renewed sense of purpose and an unshakable commitment to improve the lives of her people. She directed the Bell community redevelopment project, which enabled local citizens in a poor, rural community to build themselves a sixteen-mile (25.7km) water line and revitalize neighborhood homes.

In 1983, conservative Republican Ross Swimmer, who was running for the office of principal chief, asked her to join his ticket as deputy chief. Political differences aside, they shared an unwavering commitment to revitalizing their community. Withstanding overt sexism, harassment, and even death threats (she once answered her telephone and heard a rifle bolt being slammed shut on the other end), Mankiller was elected with Swimmer in 1983. Two years later, Swimmer was tapped to become director of the Bureau of Indian Affairs, and in accordance with tribal law, Mankiller stepped up.

Early tribal government practiced gender balance. "In 1687 women enjoyed a prominent role, but in 1987 we found people questioning whether women should be in leadership positions anywhere in the tribe," she explained when she was elected in her own right after finishing out Swimmer's term. "So my election was a step forward and step backward at the same time." Her new husband, rural development activist Charlie Soap, was especially effective. Fluent in Cherokee, he visited many homes and urged people "to not turn their backs on their past or their future." Mankiller won handily and was re-elected to a second full term in 1991. Mankiller continued to create health, education, and job programs based on a philosophy of self-help and embracing the Cherokee tradition of interconnectedness. Her legacy includes the Institute of Cherokee Literacy and the Cherokee Chamber of Commerce.

"We've managed not to just barely hang on, we've managed to move forward in a very strong, very affirmative way," said Mankiller in her 1991 inaugural address. "Given our history of adversity, I think it's a testament to our tenacity, both individually and collectively as a people, that we've been able to keep the Cherokee Nation government going since time immemorial."

Below: In 1997, Chai Ling addresses a crowd in Hong Kong in front of a banner that reads, "Don't Forget the June 4 Massacre."
Opposite: Fugitive Chai speaks to the press in Paris after surviving a harrowing escape from China.

Chai Ling
revolutionary (1966–)

After delivering an impassioned speech to the thousands of student protesters assembled in Tiananmen Square in May of 1989, firebrand Chai Ling was immediately named commander-in-chief of the student rebellion. Her words became the manifesto of the student pro-democracy movement and inspired thousands more to flock to the Beijing square. But on the night of June 3, 1989, Chinese army tanks and riot troops opened fire, massacring hundreds of people. "I could hear bullets flying and people screaming," Chai recalls. "We climbed to the upper deck of the People's Monument and could see the tanks lined up at the edge of the square. Then it was suddenly silent. We huddled together, holding hands and singing. We knew we might die, but we also felt that our sacrifice would be the most glorious in China's history."

Chai was raised in Shandon, in northeast China, by parents who were doctors for the People's Army. She was selected by the Central Communist Youth League as a "model student" while in high school. When she arrived at Beijing University to study psychology, Chai became politicized. In 1987, she joined the student movement and participated in the first demonstrations for democratic reforms in nearly forty years. On her twenty-third birthday, April 15, 1989, Chai, like thousands of others, came to Tiananmen Square to honor former Communist Party chief Hu Yaobang upon hearing the news of his death. A hero to students, he had been ousted for failing to crack down on the pro-democracy movement. As students eulogized him and increasingly criticized the regime of Deng Xiaoping, thousands decided to stay and stage a peaceful sit-in. Six weeks later, hundreds were dead and the fledgling democracy movement was crushed.

By demonstrating in Tiananmen Square, Chai and her fellow leaders forced the government to deal with them publicly, before the eyes of the world. Though they wanted to have a non-violent demonstration, they expected a violent response from the government. Believing that bloodshed was inevitable, whether in the square or through the more common method of arrest and execution, the protesters hoped that their courageous actions would inspire the masses to join the pro-democracy movement.

COURAGE OF HER CONVICTIONS

On the morning of June 4, along with her husband, Feng Congde, Chai led the last five thousand people out of the square back to the University of Beijing. Receiving word that tanks were headed there, Chai and Feng left that night and entered a harrowing ten months of hiding out in the countryside. They finally escaped, sitting silently for five days in a tiny cargo box that was nailed shut on a ship to Hong Kong, with only bread and water to sustain them. With false passports, they flew from Hong Kong to Paris, where they were granted political asylum. Feng decided to remain in Paris; Chai went on to Boston.

Continuing to speak out on issues of freedom and human rights in China, Chai hopes one day to return home. "More than anything, my strength comes from love," she said. "A love for the Chinese people—and my poor, miserable country." Having earned a master's degree from Princeton University, she divides her time between Boston, where she is a management consultant, and Washington, D.C., where she runs the China Dialogue Foundation, lobbying the U.S. government on its policy toward China.

"Freedom is a new lesson to me," she said. "I had no chance to experience it in China. I think I have to learn a lot of things about freedom. And I think freedom is painful sometimes, and that it costs a very great price."

Aung San Suu Kyi
political leader (1945–)

When Aung San Suu Kyi was awarded the Nobel Peace Prize in 1991, she did not show up to collect the award. Instead, her husband and two sons flew to Oslo to accept on her behalf because Suu Kyi, the dynamic leader of the pro-democracy movement in her native Burma, was languishing in her third year under house arrest.

Suu Kyi had been living a quiet, contented life in Oxford, England, with her husband, British professor Michael Aris, and their children when she returned to Burma (also called Myanmar) at a fateful moment. In March of 1988, Suu Kyi went back to her family's home in Rangoon to take care of her mother, who had had a stroke. That summer, thousands of protesters hit the streets to rise up against the brutal military government that had ruled by violence and intimidation for twenty-four years.

Suu Kyi felt a special connection to the cause of democracy in her country. Her father, General Aung San, was known as the "father of modern Burma," having led the movement to free the nation from British rule in the 1940s. Suu Kyi was two years old when he was assassinated, shortly before independence was achieved. She grew up learning about his courage, his legacy, and his devotion to freedom for the Burmese people. Her mother was Burma's ambassador to India; while studying there, Suu Kyi

Below: Aung San Suu Kyi after she was released from nearly six years under house arrest by Burma's military junta. **Opposite:** Defying the junta, Suu Kyi opens the first in a series of public opposition meetings, 1996.

became inspired by Mohandas Gandhi's teachings on non-violent resistance.

Suu Kyi joined the pro-democracy movement, bravely calling for the ouster of the feared dictator Ne Win in a country where critics of the regime were routinely murdered. Her speeches drew tens, even hundreds, of thousands of rapt listeners. That summer, more than three thousand protesters were killed, and Ne Win resigned, only to be replaced by the State Law and Order Restoration Council (SLORC), a military junta that promised elections but clamped down on dissidents, detaining and torturing thousands of political prisoners and executing many of its enemies.

Her mother died in December of that year, but Suu Kyi knew she had to stay. She co-founded and became the general secretary of National League for Democracy (NLD). She continued to travel around the country speaking out for democracy,

freedom, and non-violent revolution, and against SLORC's human-rights abuses—until July 19, 1989, when SLORC security forces placed her under house arrest.

Since then, Suu Kyi has been kept prisoner in her family compound more or less continually. When elections were finally held in 1990, NLD, with its beloved leader rendered invisible and silenced, nonetheless won eighty-one percent of the seats being contested. The military regime disregarded the results. In July of 1995, Suu Kyi was officially released from house arrest, but within months SLORC had again blocked off her street, restricting visitors. Her husband and now-grown sons have been allowed no more than a handful of visits.

Suu Kyi remains steadfast in her determination to achieve self-rule for her people. "We will prevail because our cause is right, because our cause is just," she said. "History is on our side. Time is on our side."

COURAGE OF HER CONVICTIONS

Chapter

4

BRIGHT IDEAS

Madam C.J. Walker, entrepreneur

Juliette Gordon Low, girls' advocate

Virginia Apgar, anesthesiologist

Simone de Beauvoir, philosopher

Gertrude Elion, chemist

Lillian Vernon, entrepreneur

Chien-Shiung Wu, nuclear physicist

Grace Hopper, computer scientist

Ellen Stewart, theater producer

Betty Friedan, writer and activist

Joan Ganz Cooney, television pioneer

Nell Merlino, communications strategist

⚬⚬⚬⚬

In one perfect moment, it all came together—a vision so clear, a concept so right, an idea so new. Creative and bold, these entrepreneurs, thinkers, and idealists brought their notions to life and made our lives that much more full.

Nell Merlino

Madam C. J. Walker

Simone de Beauvoir

Joan Ganz Cooney

Juliette Gordon Low

Lillian Vernon

Ellen Stewart

Grace Hopper

Betty Friedan

Madam C.J. Walker

entrepreneur (1867–1919)

Fortunately for Sarah Walker, who began to lose her hair at the age of thirty-eight, a "hair growing" formula came to her one night in a dream. The next morning, she ordered ingredients from around the world. She mixed the remedy and cured herself. Beginning with her savings of one dollar and fifty cents, Walker went on to parlay her own line of hair care products into a fortune; she is believed to be the first self-made U.S. woman millionaire.

Walker's product line was designed to address the specific properties of black women's hair at the turn of the century. Baldness resulting from poor diet, stress, damaging hair care treatments, and scalp diseases was common enough among black women that Walker decided to sell her products door to door. Her success was immediate, and she soon recruited hundreds of sales associates, whom she called "hair culturists," to sell her

Walker System of total hair care—shampoo, a "hair grower," vigorous brushing, and the use of hot iron combs. Although she has been criticized for advocating hairstyles that alter the natural look of black women's hair, Walker told a reporter in 1917, "Right here let me correct the erroneous impression held by some that I claim to straighten the hair. I want the great masses of my people to take a greater pride in their personal appearance and to give their hair proper attention."

The daughter of ex-slaves who were sharecroppers in the Louisiana Delta, Sarah was orphaned at the age of six. Raised by her older sister in Vicksburg, Mississippi, she began working as a domestic at ten years old. Married at fourteen and widowed at twenty, she then moved with her young daughter, A'Lelia, to St. Louis, where she worked as a washerwoman for the next eighteen years before starting her business. In 1906, she moved to Denver, Colorado, where she married journalist Charles J. Walker. By 1910, when she consolidated her business in Indianapolis, she was one of the best-known figures in America.

Despite her prominence, Booker T. Washington denied Walker the opportunity to be on the program of the 1912 National Negro Business League Convention. On the last day, she rose from her seat and addressed the mostly male audience from where she stood. "I am a woman who came from the cotton fields of the South," she began. "I was promoted from there to the washtub. Then I was promoted to the cook kitchen, and from there promoted myself into the business of manufacturing hair goods and preparations.... I have built my own factory on my own ground." Walker was invited to give the keynote speech at the next year's convention.

Walker was committed to economic independence for women—hiring former maids, teachers, farm workers, and housewives, many of whom earned in a week working for her what they had earned in a month working for others. It was her wish that her company always be run by a woman; in fact, the

Below: Millionaire Madam C.J. Walker takes the wheel, driving through Indianapolis in 1912 with her niece, personal secretary, and factory forewoman. **Opposite:** Madam C.J. Walker.

women in her family remained involved in running the business through the mid-1980s. Walker was a devoted philanthropist, giving generously to black institutions. A year before her death, Walker moved to an estate in a New York community, where she hosted meetings of black political leaders. To the very end, she was devoted to using her resources to benefit the African-American community.

Juliette Gordon Low
girls' advocate (1860–1927)

Widowed at the age of forty-four, Juliette Gordon Low found herself facing a life without direction. The eccentric Savannah socialite had been born into a life of privilege, and since marrying William Low, a wealthy fellow Georgian who lived in England, she had enjoyed a life of leisure in England and Georgia.

Finally, after several years of casting about, she met a man who helped her find her life's work at age fifty. The man was Robert Baden-Powell, the British military hero who had organized the Boy Scouts and, with his sister, Agnes, the Girl Guides in England. They became fast friends and Low became intrigued with the Girl Guides, even starting a small troop in Scotland and two in London. When she returned to the United States a year later, she called her cousin and exclaimed, "I've got something for the girls of Savannah, and all America, and all the world, and we're going to start it tonight!"

Growing up in a prominent Savannah family, Low was rambunctious, energetic, and playful. This spirited young woman burst at the seams of straight-laced Southern society. So the idea of an organization that would encourage girls to develop their whole selves thrilled her.

In March 1912, Low gathered eighteen girls to form the first troop of Girl Guides in the United States. Her dream was to focus on girls' strengths, abilities, and intelligence. Her mission: "to train girls to take their rightful places in life, first as good women, then as good citizens, wives, and mothers." The fact that "wife" and "mother" were last on the list was a radical statement for Low's time and place. Her vision was unconventional indeed. The Guides welcomed girls of all races and backgrounds, including girls with disabilities at a time when they were routinely segregated. The girls were encouraged to wear bloomers, go on camping trips, play sports, develop self-confidence, and prepare for a future in which they could pursue a profession and be involved, active citizens.

Over the next few years, Low traveled all around the country organizing troops. When the United States entered World War I, the Girl Scouts, as they had been renamed in 1913, contributed to the war effort by working in hospitals, planting vegetable gardens, and selling Liberty Bonds. This campaign helped to make the Girl Scouts a truly national movement, boasting a membership of more than eight thousand girls. Even after she retired in 1920, Low continued to promote Girl Scouting. She was never

Below: Low with two Girl Scouts early in the movement.
Opposite: Juliette Gordon Low.

seen in public without her uniform, complete with big camp hat, whistle, and tin cup at her waist. At the time of her death (she was buried in her uniform), there were almost 168,000 Girl Scouts, a number that has since swelled to nearly three million girls around the world taking their "rightful places in life."

Virginia Apgar
anesthesiologist (1909–1974)

The sounds at the moment of birth are unmistakable: a newborn's furious cry, a mother's sobs of joy, and a nurse calling out five critical numbers—the Apgar Score. Invented by Virginia Apgar, the Apgar Score evaluates the pulse, respiration, muscle tone, color, and reflexes of babies within the first moments of their lives. Used all around the world, Apgar's valuable test instantly assesses the health of the newborn and detects if an infant needs immediate medical attention.

This tall, witty woman was born and raised in Westfield, New Jersey. She majored in zoology and minored in chemistry at Mount Holyoke College while she supported herself by working odd jobs. In 1929, Apgar became one of the first women to attend Columbia University's College of Physicians and Surgeons. Upon graduation, she earned a prestigious internship in surgery at the Columbia-Presbyterian Medical Center, during which she performed two hundred operations. After recognizing that sexism would prevent her from supporting herself as a surgeon, Apgar turned to the relatively new field of anesthesiology. Here, too, she excelled. Not quite thirty years old, she became the director of the brand-new division of anesthesiology at Columbia-Presbyterian—the first woman to head a department at the medical center.

Apgar led the division for more than a decade, establishing an academic department, a staff of physician-anesthesiologists, and programs for residents and medical students. In 1949, she became the first woman to hold a full professorship at Columbia when she was appointed the first professor of anesthesiology. Much of her work was in the delivery room, and she developed a passion for making sure babies got a healthy start. Soon, Apgar left her administrative post to focus on the effects of different kinds of anesthesia on newborns. She had attended more than fifteen thousand births when she devised the Apgar Score. In what is believed to be the first significant neonatal study ever conducted in the United States, she gathered data from 1949 to 1952 to determine the criteria for medical prognoses immediately after birth. Presented in 1952, the Apgar score measures **a**ctivity (muscle tone), **p**ulse, **g**rimace (reflex irritability), **a**ppearance (skin color), and **r**espiration. It has become the universal standard to assess the health of a newborn.

In her late forties, because of her growing concern for maternal and infant health, Apgar took her career in yet another direction. Earning a master's degree in public health from Johns Hopkins University in 1959, Apgar joined the March of Dimes. She devoted the rest of her life to raising awareness and funding for research into the prevention of birth defects. In 1972, she co-authored a popular book for parents called *Is My Baby All Right?*

Apgar was a passionate and gifted teacher who was known and loved for her genuine commitment to helping people. She even carried equipment in her purse to perform emergency tracheotomies, insisting that "nobody, but nobody, is going to stop breathing on me."

Simone de Beauvoir
philosopher (1908–1986)

While teaching at a high school in Rouen, France, in her late twenties, Simone de Beauvoir was chastised by local officials for suggesting to her students that women had options other than motherhood. It wouldn't be the last time de Beauvoir raised the ire of the authorities. As an origi-

Above: Radical philosopher Simone de Beauvoir lived a life as freely independent as her thinking.

nator of existentialism and of twentieth-century feminist thought, de Beauvoir lived a life of outspoken independence.

De Beauvoir was a brilliant student, and after earning two baccalaureate degrees, she studied philosophy at the Sorbonne. There she met fellow student Jean-Paul Sartre, and they embarked on an extraordinary intellectual and romantic partnership that was to last more than fifty years. De Beauvoir was allergic to the idea of settling into a conventional domestic existence, rejecting marriage as an "unnatural institution." When she and Sartre eventually settled in Paris, they lived separately and agreed that each of them would be free to pursue "contingent" relationships with others. At age nineteen she had written, "I don't want my life to obey any other will but mine."

During World War II, de Beauvoir and Sartre participated in the French Resistance. At this time she also wrote her first novel, *She Came to Stay*, which was followed by four others. De Beauvoir and Sartre became the leading writers on existentialism, a philosophy that grapples with the ultimately inexplicable nature of human life and that stresses individual freedom of choice and responsibility for the consequences of one's acts. In her many works of fiction, philosophy, and autobiography, de Beauvoir brought a consistently biting critique of traditional bourgeois society as sterile and confining for women.

The Second Sex, which de Beauvoir published in 1949, is an exhaustively researched, compelling exploration of the idea that men have placed themselves at the center of history and society and have cast women as "the Other." "Thus," she wrote, "humanity is male and man defines woman not in herself but as relative to him; she is not regarded as an autonomous being."

For de Beauvoir, her iconoclastic writing went hand in hand with outspoken activism, and she remained committed to leftist and feminist causes throughout her life. Adamant about women's reproductive freedom, de Beauvoir founded the French pro-choice group Choisir and signed an abortion rights petition in which more than three hundred well-known women declared that they had had abortions, which were still illegal. She also supported the war for Algerian independence and worked to end the French and U.S. involvement in Vietnam.

The ideas de Beauvoir originally stated in *The Second Sex* are a cornerstone of twentieth-century feminist thought, and her personal integrity is a model that has inspired countless women and men.

Gertrude Elion
chemist (1918–)

What's amazing about Gertrude Elion is not just the number of scientific breakthroughs she has been responsible for, but the vastly different areas they are in. She discovered a treatment for childhood leukemia that has led to an eighty percent cure rate; she synthesized the anti-rejection drug that made organ transplants possible; she was responsible for a breakthrough in antiviral research when she and her team created the first effective treatment for herpes; and her research has led to treatments for gout, lupus, severe rheumatoid arthritis, malaria, and some forms of anemia and hepatitis.

The Nobel Prize Elion won in 1988 wasn't for any one of these discoveries, but rather for helping to revolutionize the *way* in which medical research is done.

The Bronx, New York-bred daughter of Eastern European Jewish immigrants, as a young woman Elion dreamed of someday making a great scientific discovery. However, when she graduated with highest honors from Hunter College with a degree in chemistry, it was 1937, and sex discrimination was perfectly

Above: Simone de Beauvoir in 1971.

Above: Gertrude Elion, whose innovative research methods earned her a Nobel Prize, at work in her lab.

legal in the United States. Not one of the fifteen universities she applied to for a graduate assistantship would give a spot to a woman. She worked marginal jobs for seven years, even working in one lab without pay for a year. During this time, she also earned her master's degree.

When World War II opened up career opportunities for women, Elion was hired as a research chemist at Burroughs Wellcome, a British pharmaceutical firm. She worked under George Hitchings, also a chemist, and together they revolutionized the nature of drug research. Instead of randomly testing chemicals' effects on diseases, they tried to create compounds specifically designed to interfere with the reproduction of disease-causing cells. Elion approached her work with complete devotion. "I was trying to prove myself because I didn't have a Ph.D.," she said, "and I felt I had to work harder because I was a woman."

In 1950, she synthesized a purine compound that interfered with the growth of leukemia cells. Used in combination with other drugs, it transformed childhood leukemia from a disease that killed most patients within months to a condition that is frequently curable.

A few years later, a variation of Elion's leukemia drug was found to suppress the immune system. This chemical, known by the trade name Imuran, made organ transplants possible by suppressing the body's natural process of rejecting a transplanted organ as a foreign substance. In 1967, Imuran was used in the first heart transplant, and it is still routinely used in kidney transplants. "When you meet someone who has lived twenty-five years with a kidney graft," said Elion, "there's your reward."

Elion's other great breakthrough came in the early 1970s, when she found a way to interfere with the reproductive process of the herpes virus. For the first time, a virus could be controlled safely with drugs.

When asked which of her many discoveries she is most proud of, she replied, "I don't discriminate among my children."

In 1988, five years after she retired, Elion was awarded the Nobel Prize for physiology or medicine, shared with Hitchings, for their basic biochemical approach to their discovery of drugs. She remains one of the very few people without a Ph.D. to win a Nobel Prize in science.

Lillian Vernon
entrepreneur (1927–)

In 1951, as a young housewife expecting her first child, Lillian Hochberg was worried about making ends meet. Hoping to earn a few extra dollars, she placed an ad in *Seventeen* magazine offering handbag and matching belt sets, personalized with the owner's initials.

To her amazement, Hochberg received thirty-two thousand dollars' worth of orders within three months. Thus was launched Vernon Specialties (named for her home in Mount Vernon, New York), later to become Lillian Vernon Corporation, the catalog company that sells affordably priced gift, household, gardening, and decorative products to the tune of $240 million a year.

ers. Her husband considered her work no more than a hobby. She couldn't get credit, so she had to pay cash up front for everything. Meanwhile, she struggled to run her household and take care of her two young sons. "Once you've dressed a struggling infant in a snowsuit, argued about the gas bill, and composed an enticing ad—all while the meatloaf bakes in the oven—the rest is a breeze," she later wrote.

Those difficult early years made Hochberg keenly aware of the needs of employed mothers. As the business expanded, she hired part-time and seasonal workers, many of whom were mothers of preschool or school-age children. "Flexible hours were and are the answer," she stated simply. Her company also offers a four-month maternity leave.

In 1968, after divorcing her husband, she legally changed her name to Lillian Vernon, a name that is now recognized by more than 43 million Americans. More than ninety percent of her customers are women. Her current catalogs showcase countless items, from the

Above: Lillian Vernon named herself and her $240 million mail order catalog company after her hometown of Mount Vernon, New York.

In those early years, she worked alone at her kitchen table, laboring feverishly to fill the orders that came pouring in. She couldn't afford an adding machine, so every Friday morning she asked her local banker if she could sit at a corner of his desk to add up her expenses and revenues for the week. In a few years, she expanded to offer items such as combs, towels, and gold-plated pins, lockets, and bookmarks, all with her trademark free monogramming.

Lillian was born to a Jewish family in Germany. After their home was seized by the Nazis, her family fled the country and started over in the United States. As a woman running her own business in the early 1950s, Hochberg faced innumerable barri-

practical (closet organizers, door mats, trivets) to the fanciful (pet placemats, sundials, Uncle Sam nutcrackers) to items that are both (personalized brass Christmas ornaments, monogrammed lint removers, bell-shaped doorstops). "I've heard people say, 'Oh, the things I like wouldn't have mass appeal,'" Vernon has written. "I consider that attitude elitist.... I do not feel that way. I'm using what I sell, decorating my home with these products."

Vernon embraces the role of responsible corporate citizen. Through her company and the Lillian Vernon Foundation, she gives money and merchandise to hundreds of causes, including help for homeless people and flood victims, wildlife protection, Jewish organizations, the arts, education, medical research, and services for the elderly. The secret to her success is simple: "Right from the start, I gave people what they wanted, at a price they could afford."

Chien-Shiung Wu
nuclear physicist (1912–)

Through meticulous research, Chien-Shiung Wu disproved a time-honored law of nature—and a time-honored assumption that women are naturally less capable than men in math and science.

Wu's early work as a researcher focused on beta decay (a type of radioactivity), and she first came to prominence as a fission expert. However, it was her experiment that disproved the law of parity—that like nuclear particles always act alike—that astounded the field of physics. This foundation of modern physics, oddly enough, had never been proven in a lab. Two young scientists, Tsung Dao Lee and Chen Ning Yang, brought this fact to Wu's attention in the 1950s. She thought that the chances of this theory proving false were one in a million, but she was intrigued by the challenge. Fiercely competitive, Wu even passed up a luxury cruise to Europe with her husband, physicist Luke Yuan, to begin work right away.

Lee and Yang wrote about their discovery that the assumption had never been proven and suggested ways to test the theory while Wu supervised the experiment. She designed a trial so complex that it took months to construct. Testing the law of parity using the equipment available in the 1950s was nothing short of extraordinary. In fact, the researchers used a potpourri of homemade bits—Ivory soap, nylon string, and crystals cooked in a beaker alongside dinner on a graduate student's stove. Incredibly, Wu and her research team discovered that nuclear particles sometimes behaved differently from each other. Lee and Yang won the 1957 Nobel Prize for physics. In a controversial decision, the Nobel Committee had decided to nominate just Lee and Yang because it was their theory, even though Wu proved it first.

Wu was born in a small town near Shanghai. An active participant in the Chinese Revolution of 1911, Wu's father was determined that his daughter would be well educated. He even founded and ran a school for girls, from which Wu graduated at nine years old. The only way she could continue her education was to attend boarding school; Wu spent the next eleven years miles away in Suzhou. She was the top student at China's prestigious National Central University in Nanjing, where she majored in physics. "If it hadn't been for my father's encouragement, I would be teaching grade school somewhere in China now," she later said.

Wu sailed from Shanghai in 1936, intending to earn her doctorate in the United States and then immediately rejoin her family. Tragically, she was not allowed to return to China for thirty-six years, and she never saw her family again.

In 1940, she earned her Ph.D. from Berkeley, but the university refused to hire her. Anti-Asian sentiments were running high in the West, and she and Yuan decided to move East. After two years of teaching at Smith College and Princeton University (where she was the first female professor), Wu joined the

Above: Chien-Shiung Wu at work in 1963 with the apparatus that conclusively proved a new and fundamental theory in nuclear physics.

Manhattan Project, which developed the first atomic bombs, thus beginning her illustrious thirty-seven-year career in the physics department of Columbia University.

"I have always felt that in physics, and probably in other endeavors, too, you must have total commitment," said Wu, who often worked in her lab until 3 or 4 a.m. "It is not just a job. It is a way of life."

Grace Hopper
computer scientist (1906–1992)

When Grace Hopper decided that she could teach computers to write programs that would translate mathematical commands into a code the computer could understand, everyone said it couldn't be done. Undaunted, the energetic, no-nonsense Hopper created the first compiler, a program that does just that. "The most damning phrase in the language is 'We've always done it this way,'" she was fond of saying. Her 1956 breakthrough paved the way for the development of programming languages.

Even as a child, she had an affinity for technology, frequently taking apart clocks. After graduating from Vassar College, she became the first woman to earn a Ph.D. in mathematics from Yale University; then she returned to Vassar to teach. During World War II, Hopper took a leave of absence to join the WAVES (Women Accepted for Volunteer Service). She became one of the world's first computer programmers, working at Harvard University on the Mark I, the first large-scale digital computer, which was being used to calculate artillery positions. This granddaddy of modern computers was a hulking fifty-one feet (15.5m) long by eight feet (2.4m) wide.

After the war, Hopper remained in the Naval reserves and taught at Harvard until 1949, when she joined the Echert-Mauchly Computer Corporation in Philadelphia. There she wrote codes for Univac I, the first commercial, large-scale, electronic computer. In the mid-1950s, Hopper became intrigued by the idea that computers could be programmed using words and phrases resembling English, not just binary ones and zeroes. "There are a lot of people who don't like symbols—they use

81

words," she recalled, "and so I said, 'Let's write the program in English, and I'll write a program that translates the English words into machine code.'"

In 1959, Hopper, along with a small group of programmers, envisioned creating a common programming language for business data processing. Their idea led to the invention of COBOL (Common Business-Oriented Language), the first dominant computer language that used an English-based vocabulary rather than a machine code. This innovation revolutionized the use of computers—what was previously a mysterious, inaccessible instrument of the military and academia became a commonplace business tool.

82

A self-professed "old-fashioned patriot," Hopper retired from the reserves in 1966. Within a year, she was recalled to active duty to oversee the standardization of the Navy's computer programs and languages. In 1983, a special presidential appointment awarded her the rank of rear admiral.

Held in high esteem by her peers, Hopper was granted numerous awards for her pioneering work, including the National Medal of Technology, and has been memorialized by the Grace Hopper Celebration of Women in Computing, a technical conference focusing on the achievements of women in the field.

When she retired (reluctantly) from the Navy for good in 1986 after forty-three years of service, she was the oldest officer and the last of the World War II WAVES to leave active duty. Despite her long years of service in the military, she hated bureaucracy. "I tell everybody, go ahead and do it," she said. "You can always apologize later."

Ellen Stewart
theater producer (1919–)

The maverick mother of avant-garde theater, Ellen Stewart has a very strict criterion for deciding whether she'll produce a play. "If a play is talking to me personally," she explains, "if a script *beeps* to me when I'm reading it, we do it." Her intuition is uncanny. As founder and director of La MaMa Experimental Theater Club (E.T.C.) in New York City, she has discovered and nurtured a stunning array of world-renowned playwrights, directors, and actors, and La MaMa E.T.C. has presented more than eighteen hundred productions. Stewart's greatest gift, however, may be her tireless, passionate efforts to bring together cultures from every corner of the globe, making her one of the strongest influences in the world arts community.

Several members of Stewart's family were on the vaudeville circuit and in the circus. When her foster brother needed a place to put on his plays, she reached back to that tradition and opened Café La MaMa in 1961 in a rented basement theater on New York City's Lower East Side. "Theater was in my blood," says Stewart. "Nor was it traditional, text-based theater. It was body language, music, dance. Theater for me is energy; it is sensual, spontaneous.... La MaMa made use of this heritage. We developed new means of expression rooted in something ancient." Unconventional in its form and style, the newly emerging avant-garde genre appealed to Stewart; young people working in experimental theater flocked to Café La MaMa, where their artistic vision was welcomed. Rechristened La MaMa Experimental Theater Club, the organization got a permanent home in 1968, when Stewart purchased a building with a grant from the Ford Foundation. La MaMa E.T.C. currently operates three small experimental theater spaces, rehearsal rooms, and an art gallery; Stewart lives on the top floor.

No critics would come to the club in the 1960s, however, so in 1965, Stewart sent her troupe and twenty-two of their plays to Europe to establish a reputation for La MaMa's artists. That was the beginning of her commitment to work internationally. La MaMa productions have gone abroad every year since then; there are La MaMa troupes in France, Israel, Turkey, Japan, and Italy. Stewart herself travels around the world, seeking out and

bringing the finest productions back to her modest theater. La MaMa's thirty-fifth anniversary season included a Bulgarian *Medea*, a Croatian *Moon Over Alabama*, a Kabuki Kanadehon *Hamlet*, a Czech *Golem* performed by century-old puppets, and a Greek *Phaedra*. In 1985, Stewart received a MacArthur "genius" award, which she used to establish La MaMa Umbria, an artists' residence in Spoleto, Italy.

She has been criticized (and denied significant funding) for not being American enough as well as for not doing enough specifically for African Americans, but Stewart has a much larger vision. "I think in world terms," she explains. "I believe we are one race, and everybody is in that race. And one day we are going to learn to trust what is within us, so that we can be in tune with the world, the earth, the moon, the stars, the universe."

Betty Friedan
writer (1921 –)

The problem lay buried, unspoken, for many years in the minds of American women. It was a strange stirring, a sense of dissatisfaction, a yearning that women suffered in the middle of the twentieth century in the United States.

Above: Betty Friedan speaks at a 1983 banquet in her honor celebrating the twentieth anniversary of her book, *The Feminine Mystique.* **Below:** Betty Friedan and Gloria Steinem sign a telegram urging President Carter to support the Equal Rights Amendment, 1977.

So began an unparalleled chapter in the history of women's lives as Betty Friedan exposed the "problem that has no name" in her 1963 landmark book, *The Feminine Mystique.* Friedan articulated a previously vague lack of self-fulfillment experienced by hundreds of thousands of suburban, middle-class house-wives who could not use their talent and education outside the home. The book clearly touched a nerve; it was eventually translated into thirteen languages and sold three million copies.

Born Betty Goldstein in Peoria, Illinois, she graduated with honors from Smith College. After one year of graduate school, she moved to New York City for a newspaper

career and soon married adman Carl Friedan. She became a housewife in suburban Rockland County, New York, and raised three children while continuing as a freelance writer.

Gradually she found herself bored, in need of greater stimulation and challenge. On the occasion of the fifteen-year reunion of her Smith class, she circulated a questionnaire among her classmates. The results suggested that they too were dissatisfied with their roles. Friedan got an advance from publisher W.W. Norton to do broader research for a book. *The Feminine Mystique*—which contended that the dominant post–World War II ideology of women's fulfillment through domesticity had become a trap for middle-class women—became an immediate best-seller and propelled Friedan to national visibility.

In 1966, she co-founded and became the first president of the National Organization for Women (NOW), whose goal was "to bring women into full participation in the mainstream of American society *now*, exercising all the privileges and responsibilities thereof in truly equal partnership with men." NOW, which eventually grew to 300,000 members, has remained a leading force in the movement for the Equal Rights Amendment, equal pay, access to child care, and reproductive rights.

Friedan, meanwhile, became increasingly disturbed at what she perceived as the dominance of radical feminists. In her 1976 book, *It Changed My Life*, and 1981's *The Second Stage*, she argued against "sexual politics" and deplored the women's movement's focus on "racism, poverty, rape, and lesbian rights" as alienating to the mainstream. She warned against attacks on men, marriage, and the family. Other feminists, in turn, criticized Friedan for misinterpreting feminism's condemnation of male supremacy as personally attacking men. Still others opposed Friedan's repudiation of feminism as a broad-based, multi-issue, multiconstituency movement that should address issues of class, race, and sexuality.

In 1993's *The Fountain of Age*, Friedan turned her attention to an upbeat re-envisioning of aging, reframing what she had once approached with dread as an opportunity for growth and expanding possibilities. The influence of her first book, however, remains her crowning achievement and a watershed in the lives of countless women.

Above: Joan Ganz Cooney in 1973.

Joan Ganz Cooney
television pioneer (1929–)

*I*n 1968, Joan Ganz Cooney envisioned something never before seen on television—an innovative, lively, multicultural television program that would teach basic language, reasoning, and moral concepts to preschool children. Thirty years later, *Sesame Street* is still beloved and watched by millions of children and parents in more than eighty-five countries. The program delights toddlers and grownups alike with its clever parodies, intelligent humor, and timeless sketches.

After graduating from the University of Arizona, Joan Ganz started out as a reporter in her hometown of Phoenix. Having raised their daughter in an upper-middle-class, traditional Roman Catholic home, her parents were alarmed when she decided to move to New York City to pursue a career in public

daily television program could indeed educate the large target audience of urban, disadvantaged preschoolers. Remarkably, her original vision—short, fast-paced segments featuring a mix of animation, live action, and puppets; a racially diverse cast; repetitive concepts; "commercials" for letters and numbers; music and comedy, all set on an urban tenement street—is still the core of *Sesame Street*'s magic today.

Sesame Street was researched and developed for more than two years before it premiered on November 10, 1969, under the auspices of the newly founded Children's Television Workshop (CTW). The show was soon attracting an audience of seven million preschoolers—an unprecedented number of viewers for public television. In 1970, *Sesame Street* won Emmy and Peabody awards, and it has earned countless honors since.

Cooney served as CTW's president and chief executive officer until 1990. In addition to *Sesame Street*, Cooney and her colleagues created the children's programs *The Electric Company*, *3-2-1 Contact*, *Square One TV*, *Ghostwriter*, and *CRO*. Cooney has received numerous awards for her pioneering vision, including a Daytime Emmy for Lifetime Achievement and the Presidential Medal of Freedom, the United States's highest civilian honor. Of her working style, she said, "I like to feel I am a hardheaded business woman, but I suppose underneath it all I am still a crusader. I would like to bring about change for the better."

Above: Cooney and her furry friends from Sesame Street.
Opposite: Take Our Daughters to Work creator Nell Merlino in 1993.

relations. She remembers her mother's reaction: "When I left Arizona, she said, 'You know, you are a big fish in a little pond in Phoenix; why do you want to be a little fish in a big pond?' I said, 'How do you know I won't be a big fish in a big pond?'"

Cooney (in 1964 she married Tim Cooney, with whom she stayed for eleven years) was already an award-winning public affairs producer for New York's public television station, WNET/Thirteen, when the Carnegie Corporation asked her to conduct a feasibility study on using television to educate young children. Cooney traveled throughout the country gathering ideas from educators and child experts. She also looked at children's television viewing patterns and noticed that kids were more responsive to fast-paced commercials with snappy jingles than to regular programming. In a few months, Cooney had written her report, concluding that an hour-long, well-made

Nell Merlino
communications strategist (1953–)

Imagine a spring day in New York City. It is rush hour and every other adult is accompanied by a girl on the subway. Elevators and cafeterias are jammed with little girls and their parents, mentors or Big Sisters. Take Our Daughters to Work Day will take girls out of their usual settings where they are often ignored, and bring them into public focus.

ith this brilliantly simple idea, Nell Merlino galvanized more than one million people on behalf of girls.

Alarmed by mounting evidence that the self-esteem of girls tends to plummet as they approach adolescence, the Ms.

Foundation for Women, a nonprofit feminist organization, turned to Merlino for a creative way to focus the public's attention on this disturbing phenomenon. Merlino conceived of Take Our Daughters to Work (TODTW) day.

On April 28, 1993, girls were everywhere. Girls traded pizza futures on the floor of the Chicago Mercantile Exchange, they climbed into cherry pickers at the Tennessee Valley Authority, they tested space equipment at NASA, they ran households with homemakers. Images of girls—competent, inquisitive, and excited—were on the front pages of every major American newspaper and national broadcast news program. Even if just for a day, girls were, in Merlino's words, "visible, valued, and heard."

The daughter of a genteel artist and a powerful former New Jersey state senator, Merlino has an unusually creative mind and the guts to turn her ideas into action. She thought of the idea for TODTW at the retirement party for her father, whom she had often accompanied to work as a girl.

After graduating from Antioch College, Merlino began working in the labor movement, organizing health care workers; at twenty-five, she won a Fulbright Scholarship to study labor relations in England. When she returned, she spent ten years working in government, including time as an advance person for the presidential campaigns of Walter Mondale and Michael Dukakis. The bureaucratic pace proved too slow and cumbersome for the energetic Merlino. In 1989, she founded her own company, Strategy Communication Action Ltd., to produce "media-genic" public initiatives.

A recent poll found that 15.4 million adults said that they or their spouses personally brought a girl to work on TODTW day. "What continues to astound me is how much each group of girls that enters this age range needs this," said Merlino. The lasting impact of TODTW will be felt in the next ten years as millions of girls who participated in the campaign pursue their dreams.

"All the work I've done has been about mobilizing people," said Merlino. And no issue is too big or too complex; Merlino has designed campaigns to fight AIDS, preserve the environment, dismantle patriarchy, and eliminate violence. Brash and charismatic, she is a formidable presence in any crowd. Her advice to girls is "to have confidence in what you think, to say what you think, and to spend as much time thinking about how you're going to make a living as you do worrying about what you look like."

ONE OF A KIND

Carry Nation, reformer

Emma Goldman, anarchist

Gertrude Stein, writer

Alice Paul, suffragist

Nadia Boulanger, teacher and conductor

Virginia Woolf, writer

Zora Neale Hurston, folklorist and anthropologist

Frida Kahlo, artist

Billie Holiday, jazz singer

Katharine Hepburn, actor

Eva Perón, first lady

Julia Child, chef

Toni Morrison, writer

Madonna, singer and actor

———————— ∞ ————————

Impossible to categorize, these individuals are true originals—each following her own path, whether it be one of genius, outrageousness, or eccentricity.

Gertrude Stein

Billie Holiday

Virginia Woolf

Katharine Hepburn

Carry Nation

Nadia Boulanger

Emma Goldman

Eva Peron

Frida Kahlo

Carry Nation
reformer (1846–1911)

Swinging a hatchet and singing a hymn, prohibitionist Carry Nation took matters into her own hands by smashing up saloons at the turn of the century. Widowed within a few years of her marriage to an alcoholic, she had made it her personal mission to eradicate the evil of alcohol. With religious fervor, the self-described "destroyer of the works of the Devil by the direct order of God" closed countless saloons and achieved national notoriety.

Throughout her childhood, her family moved back and forth between Kentucky, Missouri, and Texas, finally settling in Missouri. Her mother was mentally ill and believed she was Queen Victoria of England; Carry's father humored his wife by pretending to be Prince Albert. Young Carry was sickly and attended school sporadically. She underwent her first religious awakening at the age of ten; she would experience deep spiritual anxiety alternating with extreme emotional elation throughout her life.

After the death of her husband, she supported herself and her baby daughter by teaching. In 1877, she married the much-older David Nation, a journalist and lawyer who dabbled in the ministry. They eventually moved to Medicine Lodge, Kansas. Although Kansas had been a legally "dry" state since 1880, thinly disguised "joints" nevertheless continued to serve alcohol. In 1892, Nation co-founded the county chapter of the Woman's Christian Temperance Union to preach against the evils of drinking. To her way of thinking the problem clearly lay with undisciplined men. As she wrote in her autobiography, *The Use and Need of the Life of Carry A. Nation* (1905), "The success of life, the formation of character, is in proportion to the courage one has to say to one's own self: 'Thou shalt not.'"

In 1899, Nation had a vision in which God told her to go, weapon in hand, to close down a saloon. The six-foot-tall, exceptionally strong woman filled the doorway of the Dodson Saloon. With tears streaming down her face, singing a temperance song, Nation threw bricks and swung a hatchet, destroying tables, mirrors, glasses, and bottles, forcing the saloon to close. News of her attack spread quickly, and similar actions soon dried up the whole town. Looking for volunteers to join her smashing crusade, or "hatchetation," as she called it, Nation said, "This appeal is made to the gentle, loving brave Christian women whose hearts are breaking with sympathy for the oppressed.... Bring your hatchet." Although she frequently escaped harm because of her gender, she was attacked, beaten, and humiliated several times. She was arrested more than thirty-three times and spent a total of 170 days in jail.

Vigilante groups similar to hers sprang up around the country, and Nation received thousands of small donations from

Below: A town marshall in Enterprise, Kansas, leads Carry Nation away after she destroyed a saloon in 1911. **Opposite:** Nation, with her tools in hand—hatchet and Bible.

90

ONE OF A KIND

ONE OF A KIND

individuals. Most of the money went to pay her jail fines and to support her national lecture tour. She traveled from coast to coast, preaching and selling her autobiography and thousands of miniature hatchets with the engraving, "Carry Nation, Joint Smasher." She even briefly appeared as a sideshow attraction at Coney Island. Her husband divorced her in 1901 on the grounds of desertion. She collapsed on a stage in Arkansas in 1910 and died several months later. Her gravestone reads, "She Hath Done What She Could."

Below: Standing in a car, Emma Goldman courageously advocates for birth control in a sea of men at Union Square Park in New York City, 1916. **Opposite:** Emma Goldman (left) in 1934.

Emma Goldman
anarchist (1869–1940)

Working in a clothing factory in Rochester, New York, for two dollars and fifty cents a week, young Russian émigré Emma Goldman was appalled at the exploitation of immigrant workers through long workdays, low pay, and terrible living conditions. She heard about the newly burgeoning anarchist movement, which identified capitalism as the culprit and revolution as the remedy for the plight of exploited workers, and in 1889 she moved to New York City to become a revolutionary.

Goldman was captivated by the ideal of a community of individuals free from the controls of private property, government, and religion. She dreamed of a society of small, non-hierarchical groups of people who would be free to determine their own needs and fulfill them in a spirit of cooperation, equality, and justice.

In New York, she met Alexander Berkman, a young Russian radical who would become her lover briefly and her friend and comrade for the next forty-five years. Early on, she embraced the idea of violence as a means to revolution and even helped Berkman plot the assassination of Henry Clay Frick, the chairman of Carnegie Steel. In 1892, Berkman was sentenced to twenty-two years in prison for his attempt (he served fourteen). The following year, Goldman herself was arrested for telling a crowd of unemployed men and women that it was their "sacred right" to steal bread if they were starving. In prison, Goldman rethought her stance and rejected violence as a means for social change. "Methods and means cannot be separated from the ultimate aim," she realized.

Goldman embarked on lecture tours in the United States and Europe and soon became known as a fiery, brilliant, and persuasive orator. She scandalized most segments of the public but thrilled budding revolutionaries by advocating the abolition of church and state, equality of the sexes, homosexuality, birth control, free speech, and free love. "Love, the strongest and deepest element in all life, the harbinger of hope, of joy, of ecstasy," she wrote, "how can such an all-compelling force be synonymous with that poor little State- and Church-begotten weed, marriage?" With Berkman, she published the radical monthly *Mother Earth* for ten years.

Goldman was repeatedly arrested for the things she said. She and Berkman both opposed U.S. involvement in World War I, and in 1917 they were sentenced to two years in prison for their vehement denunciation of the newly instituted military draft. When they were released in September of 1919, the United States was in the midst of a big Red Scare, and "Red Emma," as she was inaccurately nicknamed, along with Berkman and several hundred other "subversives," was deported to the Soviet Union. Disgusted by the brutality of the Bolshevik regime, she soon moved to Sweden, where she wrote *My Disillusionment with Russia*.

Goldman spent the rest of her life mostly in Europe, where she continued to lecture against war and repression. Her autobiography, *Living My Life*, was published in 1931. At the end of her life, she was still fighting the good fight, this time for the antifascist forces of the Spanish Civil War. "One cannot be too extreme in dealing with social ills," she wrote. "Besides, the extreme thing is generally the true thing." Goldman's courage in daring to speak out about her unconventional beliefs, even in the face of jail and deportation, has inspired generations.

Gertrude Stein
writer (1874–1946)

"Einstein was the creative philosophic mind of the century, and I have been the creative literary mind of the century." This was Gertrude Stein's less-than-understated assessment of her vast, varied, and innovative body of work.

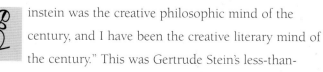

ly salons at their home, which became a famous gathering place for leading intellectuals, artists, and writers throughout the 1920s.

In 1907, Stein met Alice B. Toklas, daughter of a wealthy San Francisco family. Toklas recognized Stein's genius and the two women became lovers and companions, living together until Stein's death. Toklas ran the household, typed all of Stein's manuscripts, and eventually managed her business affairs.

Stein wrote daily for almost fifty years, creating plays, operas, novels, essays, poetry, and autobiographies. As a writer, Stein embraced the experimental approach that she valued in painting, viewing her work as a literary parallel to Cubism or abstraction. Her writing was challenging, if not unintelligible, to a popular audience. Stein was unperturbed by this, saying, "My work would have been no use to anyone if the public had understood me at first." Often she would have to wait years for a work to be published. She played with language, with the sounds and juxtapositions of words. She created fascinating rhythms and rhymes and broke the rules of form, grammar, and punctuation. There was sometimes a deceptive simplicity in her work; she is known for such lines as "Rose is a rose is a rose" and "Pigeons in the grass alas."

Above: Gertrude Stein relaxes in her Paris home under Pablo Picasso's portrait of her. **Right:** In 1944, Stein and her life partner, Alice B. Toklas, stroll with their dog, "Basket," down the lane in the French village where they lived during the Nazi occupation of France.

Born in Allegheny, Pennsylvania, Stein was the youngest of five children of German Jewish immigrants. She spent her early years in Vienna and Paris, until the family settled in Oakland, California, when she was five. After her parents died, her inheritance left her comfortable, if not wealthy. She attended Radcliffe, then Johns Hopkins Medical School. She lost interest in medicine and finally settled in Paris in 1903 with her older brother Leo.

Stein and her brother started collecting the paintings of then-little-known artists such as Cézanne, Gauguin, Renoir, Picasso, and Matisse; Stein became a champion of the Cubists and other contemporary artists. The Steins started holding week-

ONE OF A KIND

Her first published book, *Three Lives*, a collection of short stories about three working-class women, was well-received. *Tender Buttons*, a volume of Cubist prose poems, is an extremely abstract, difficult work. Stein also wrote librettos for two operas, *Four Saints in Three Acts* (which is not about four saints and is not presented in three acts) and *Mother of Us All*, based on the life of Susan B. Anthony, as well as critical works, including *Composition as Explanation* and *How to Write*.

In 1933, she published *The Autobiography of Alice B. Toklas*, which was actually Stein's memoir written in Toklas' voice. Funny and accessible, it was immediately a popular success. Stein was rather unnerved by the enthusiastic reception; she had accepted the fact that her work was beyond the reach of most readers. As she wrote, "Nobody knows what I am trying to do but I do and I know when I succeed."

Above: With a glass of grape juice, Alice Paul toasts the state of Tennessee as it ratifies the Suffrage Amendment in 1920.

Alice Paul
suffragist (1885–1977)

In her unwavering campaign for women's suffrage, Alice Paul gave new meaning to the term single-minded. She was imprisoned for her spirited protests and went on hunger strikes that endangered her health. It was said that she never read about topics other than women's suffrage, so as not to be distracted. She was often so obsessed with the work at hand that even her ardent supporters found her rude and insensitive. But Paul revitalized the United States suffrage movement when it was flagging, and the spark of her passion for women's equality lit a fire under thousands of activists for generations.

Paul was raised in the Quaker religion, which affirms the equality of women and men; growing up with this belief surely fueled her later sense of outrage when she encountered gender injustice. After graduating from Swarthmore College near

Philadelphia and earning a master's degree in sociology at the University of Pennsylvania, she was awarded a fellowship to study social work in Woodbridge, England.

It was in England that Paul was radicalized. When she attended a speech by the fiery Christabel Pankhurst, leader along with her mother, Emmeline, of the militant "suffragettes," Paul was turned on to the movement's zeal. The suffragettes' tactics—including noisy demonstrations, sabotage, defacement of public property, and arson—drew plenty of attention to the cause of women's suffrage and frequently landed the activists in prison. Captivated by their vision and sense of urgency, Paul worked alongside the Pankhursts for two years.

When she returned to the United States in 1910, she found a suffrage movement that was stalled, ineffective, and far too decorous. In 1912, Paul took over the leadership of the National

American Woman Suffrage Association's Congressional Committee. Before long she and her supporters split off to form the Congressional Union for Woman Suffrage, and later the National Woman's Party. Taking her cue from the British suffragettes, Paul adopted a militant approach that outraged suffrage opponents and horrified her more moderate feminist sisters. In 1913, when marches on Washington were unheard of, she organized a demonstration in which five thousand women marched down Pennsylvania Avenue in Washington, D.C., on the day before President Woodrow Wilson's inauguration. In 1917, she organized the first group of suffragists to picket the White House. She and her followers were thrown in jail, went on hunger strikes to protest their treatment, and underwent agonizing force-feedings. Extensive publicity got them attention and some sympathy.

On August 26, 1920, President Wilson signed into law the Nineteenth Amendment, ensuring all American women the right to vote. It was the culmination of countless hours of dedicated work by hundreds of thousands of women and men for more than a century. For Paul, it was the beginning of a new phase of activism. Within three years she drafted a federal Equal Rights Amendment and got it introduced into Congress. She continued to work for passage of the ERA until her death in 1977. "Well, I always thought once you put your hand on the plough," she said, "you don't remove it until you get to the end of the row."

Nadia Boulanger
teacher and conductor (1887–1979)

*T*he teacher of virtually every major American composer from 1929 to 1940, Nadia Boulanger inspired the likes of Aaron Copland, Virgil Thomson, Eliot Carter, Roy Harris, Walter Piston, and George Gershwin to greatness.

Boulanger drove her students hard, with almost religious fervor, imposing strict discipline. "Great art likes chains," she said. "The greatest artists have created art within bounds. Or else they have created their own chains." She demanded nothing short of perfection from her students; her zeal awakened in them the passion and drive to achieve superior artistry.

Above: Nadia Boulanger. **Opposite:** Virginia Woolf and her father, Sir Leslie Stephen, circa 1900.

Born into a family of musicians, Boulanger took her first music lessons as a young child from her mother, a Russian countess and professional singer. At age ten, she began attending the Paris Conservatory, where her father and grandfather taught. She studied composition with the renowned organist and composer Gabriel Fauré, who, along with her friend Igor Stravinsky, became the major influence on her career. At the conservatory, she won first prizes in harmony, counterpoint, fugue, organ, and accompaniment. At age twenty-one, she won a prestigious Prix de Rome for her cantata *La Sirène.*

Her younger sister, Lili, who was an exceptionally gifted and promising composer, died in 1919 at the age of twenty-five. Deeply affected by Lili's death, Boulanger stopped writing music altogether and poured her heart and talent into teaching. Her illustrious teaching career had begun at the Paris Conservatory in 1909, and she later taught at the Ecole Normale de Musique in Paris.

Boulanger established her reputation as a brilliant teacher of composition primarily at the American Conservatory in Fontainebleau, where she taught from 1921 and directed from 1950.

While American composers traveled to Paris to study with her (Copland later described her tutelage as the most important musical experience of his life), Boulanger dazzled Americans as a guest performer, conductor, and teacher. She played the organ part in Copland's *Organ Symphony* with the New York Symphony Orchestra (1925); she was the first woman to conduct the Boston Symphony Orchestra (1938) and the New York Philharmonic (1939). As a conductor, she was a pioneer in the performance of French Baroque and Renaissance music.

Boulanger remained in the United States throughout World War II, teaching classes at Radcliffe College, Wellesley College, and the Julliard School of Music. In 1946, she went home to Paris and the American Conservatory. Boulanger was revered in high society; she selected and conducted the musical program at the wedding of the Prince of Monaco and Grace Kelly in 1956.

Admired for her exhaustive knowledge of a vast body of music, her intuition about the essence of a new musical idea, and her sensitivity to rhythm and phrasing in performance, Boulanger is considered one of the greatest teachers of modern times. "It is nothing to succeed if one has not taken great trouble," she said, "and it is nothing to fail if one has done the best one could."

Virginia Woolf
writer (1882–1941)

'm fundamentally, I think, an outsider," wrote Virginia Woolf in her diary in 1938. "I do my best work and feel most braced with my back to the wall. It's an odd feeling though, writing against the current: difficult entirely to disregard the current. Yet of course I shall." Woolf consistently wrote and lived against the current, creating enduring works of literature and criticism.

She was born Adeline Virginia Stephen; her father was a prominent London editor and critic who, consistent with the custom of the day, denied his daughters a formal education. Virginia became educated by helping herself to her father's extensive library and through sporadic private tutoring. Her mother died when Virginia was thirteen, and the girl plunged into the first of several bouts of major depression that she was to suffer throughout her life.

After their father died in 1904, Virginia and her sister, Vanessa, and brothers, Thoby and Adrian, moved to 46 Gordon Square, in the Bloomsbury section of London. Their home functioned as the center of what came to be called the Bloomsbury Group, a circle of avant-garde artists, critics, writers, and intellectuals who helped to create the twentieth-century modernist movement in art and literature, and whose influence is still felt.

In 1912, she married leftist journalist Leonard Woolf, although she felt ambivalent about marriage and about him as a partner; nonetheless, he was loving and supportive. Together they founded the Hogarth Press, which published the work of

Woolf herself and other modern writers, including T.S. Eliot and Katherine Mansfield.

Woolf's first novel, *The Voyage Out*, was published in 1915. Later she started to experiment, departing from the strict plot structure and length of the Victorian novel. Subtle, nonlinear, and impressionistic, her fiction helped to define modernist literature. She experimented with poetic devices, time frames, and point of view in her best-known novels, *Mrs. Dalloway* (1925), *To the Lighthouse* (1927), and *The Waves* (1931), which is a stream-of-consciousness work whose perspective stays within the minds of the six characters. Woolf was also a highly respected literary critic.

In 1929, Woolf published *A Room of One's Own*, a brilliant exploration of the social constraints that plague women artists. "A woman must have money and a room of her own if she is to write fiction," Woolf argued. Her observations have proven to be timeless, and *A Room of One's Own* is a feminist classic.

Today, Woolf is as well-known for her lengthy diaries, which detail the daily life and relationships of her family and friends and chronicle her quixotic moods; and her letters, hundreds of which have been published. In 1919, she determined that her diary would be "so elastic that it will embrace anything, solemn, slight or beautiful that comes into my mind."

In 1941, suffering from depression, Woolf committed suicide by filling her pockets with stones and walking into the River Ouse near her home. Her final novel, *Between the Acts*, was published posthumously.

Zora Neale Hurston
folklorist and anthropologist (c. 1901–1960)

The small town of Eatonville, Florida, filled with flowing rivers and juicy guavas and black folks telling colorful tales, was the rich soil from which folklorist Zora Neale Hurston sprang and where she returned to cultivate her most memorable characters. One of the brightest stars of the Harlem Renaissance, Hurston left a fascinating and contradictory legacy. Her behavior and politics were unpredictable, her fans and her critics were likely to come from any race and either

gender, and her writings have been both popular and obscure in her lifetime and after her death. She was undoubtedly a gifted novelist, essayist, playwright, anthropologist, folklorist, and social critic.

Hurston's father was a preacher and the mayor of Eatonville, the first all-black incorporated township in America. Young Zora thrived in the bosom of this ground-breaking community, growing up self-possessed and proud of her culture. She was well educated by the local teachers and encouraged by her mother, Lucy. "Mama exhorted her children at every opportunity to 'jump at de sun,'" Hurston wrote. "We might not land on the sun, but at least we would get off the ground." When Hurston was thirteen years old, her mother's death and her father's hasty remarriage shattered her childhood, and she described her subsequent years as "a series of wanderings," in which she worked menial jobs.

Hurston landed in New York in 1925 and earned an anthropology degree from Barnard College, becoming the school's first black graduate. Further study under the renowned anthropologist Franz Boas convinced Hurston that there was a wider audience for the people and stories of her childhood. She returned to the South to research her book *Mules and Men*, the first history of black folklore by a black writer.

Setting her novels squarely in all-black environs, Hurston created a space where her characters could laugh loudly, speak in lush rhythms, and live their own lives. White people and racism hover around the outskirts, their presence felt but not elaborated upon. Her beautifully written second novel, 1934's *Their Eyes Were Watching God*, the story of protagonist Janie Starks' search for self-fulfillment, is an enduring classic.

Hurston's studies and writing were often made possible by the patronage of white people, although she was angered that her patrons could control her work. Pressured into writing her autobiography, Hurston reluctantly produced the infamously evasive *Dust Tracks on a Road* in 1943. Around this time, she moved back to Florida, bought a houseboat, and spent much of the mid-1940s sailing Florida waters. Her writing got further away from her folkloric roots, and her popularity waned. She worked again as a maid and did freelance writing, struggling to make a living.

All of Hurston's books were out of print in 1960, when she died from a stroke in a Florida welfare home. In the mid-1970s, writer Alice Walker uncovered Hurston's unmarked grave and her abundant body of work. Walker edited an anthology of Hurston's writings entitled *I Love Myself When I Am Laughing, and Also When I Am Mean and Impressive*, allowing entire new generations to taste the bittersweet fruit of Zora Neale Hurston.

Frida Kahlo
artist (1907–1954)

While recovering from massive injuries suffered in a bus accident as a teenager in 1925, Frida Kahlo taught herself to paint. Her strikingly vivid style caught the eye of Mexican muralist Diego Rivera, who urged her to continue. Kahlo did, pouring her pain and grief onto the canvas as she endured a lifetime of operations. Her intense self-portraits with searingly raw emotions laid bare in brilliant colors are often shocking and painful to behold, but Kahlo created some of the most indelible artistic images of this century. "They thought I was a Surrealist, but I wasn't," Kahlo insisted. "I never painted dreams. I painted my reality."

Her reality was tragic at best. At the age of six, Kahlo was stricken with polio. After a yearlong convalescence, one of her legs remained smaller and thinner than the other. When she was eighteen, a bus drove head-on into the trolley she was riding on, and her body was shattered. Her abdomen was torn open by a handrail, her pelvis fractured, her spine broken in several places, and her right leg and foot crushed. She had to undergo thirty-five operations over the years. Her physical and emotional trauma fed her work and was usually its subject: many of her paint-

Below: Frida Kahlo frequently painted herself, as here in *Self-Portrait with Monkey*, 1940. **Opposite:** Harlem Renaissance luminary Zora Neale Hurston in 1950.

ONE OF A KIND

ings express her rage at her disabilities, her stormy marriage to Rivera, and her inability to bear a child.

Refusing to be categorized by art critics, the gifted Kahlo said, "I put on the canvas whatever comes into my mind." Drawing on the rich tradition and primitive style of Mexican folk art, Kahlo integrated fantastical elements and bright colors into her work, which consisted primarily of self-portraits. Her provocative images, new to the Western art world, included visible internal organs, cross-dressing, and explicit portrayals of birth and miscarriages.

Kahlo had met Rivera, whom she considered the greatest painter in the world, when he was commissioned to paint a mural at her high school. Married in 1929, the couple divorced in 1939 and remarried two years later, surviving tempestuous quarrels and numerous affairs (Rivera slept with Kahlo's sister; Kahlo took up with Leon Trotsky, among other men and

women). Profoundly conflicted about her feelings for her husband, she once wrote to him, "I love you more than my own skin." However, she later said, "I suffered two grave accidents in my life. One in which a streetcar knocked me down.... The other accident is Diego." Kahlo suffered three miscarriages and was bitterly disappointed that she could not give birth to a child. One of her miscarriages coincided with her mother's death in 1932, while Kahlo was working on a painting called *My Birth*. This stark painting peers between her mother's legs at the moment of Frida's birth; her mother's head is covered in a shroud.

In the early 1930s, Kahlo traveled throughout the United States with Rivera, who had been commissioned by several American cities to paint murals. While Rivera was more famous, he consistently supported Kahlo's artistry and advocated for her to be recognized in her own right. In the 1940s, she began to exhibit internationally. In 1943, she was appointed a professor of painting at Mexico's Education Ministry's School of Fine Arts. Her last few years of life were again plagued with illness; she was carried in on a stretcher to attend her first major solo exhibition in Mexico. Strong-willed to the end, she said, "I am happy to be alive, as long as I can paint."

Billie Holiday
jazz singer (1915–1959)

No one could sing like Billie Holiday. She would wrap her voice around a melody and shape it into something utterly unique. For more than twenty-five years, she mesmerized audiences with her heartfelt, inventive interpretations, leaving a legacy of hundreds of recordings and a troubled life.

She never had it easy. Billie was born to teenage parents in a Baltimore ghetto. Her father left when she was a child; soon thereafter, her mother moved to New York to work as a maid, leaving Billie with relatives. She was not quite ten years old when she started doing chores for a brothel keeper, who allowed her to hang out and listen to recordings of blues and jazz greats like Bessie Smith and Louis Armstrong.

She dropped out of school after fifth grade to join her mother in New York. Although Holiday had no formal musical training,

Above: Billie Holiday, wearing a trademark gardenia in her hair, croons a jazz tune. **Opposite:** Frida Kahlo in 1944.

ONE OF A KIND

by the time she was sixteen she was singing in Harlem night-clubs. She made a number of recordings with Teddy Wilson and his band, whose loose, instinctive approach complemented her fluid style. "I can't stand to sing the same song the same way two nights in succession, let alone two years or ten years," she said. "If you can, then it ain't music, it's close-order drill or exercise or yodeling or something, not music." In 1935, she debuted at the famous Apollo Theater in Harlem. "Lady Day," as she came to be known, had hit the big time.

After successful tours with Count Basie and with Artie Shaw, Holiday started appearing at the posh Café Society in New York City, where she created a sensation with her memorable interpretations of two songs that would become her trademarks: "God Bless the Child" and "Strange Fruit," a haunting song about lynching. Throughout the early 1940s, she was in great demand, performing in New York and many other cities and enjoying a thriving recording career.

Despite her success, she had to put up with the indignities and humiliations of racism. She once had to enter a hotel where she was performing through the kitchen. Some clubs barred her from performing with Artie Shaw's all-white ensemble. Her label, Columbia, wouldn't even allow her to record "Strange Fruit," which was unusually direct in its description of racist violence. When she was cast in a film in 1946, it was not as a performer but as a maid.

Meanwhile, Holiday's personal life was a mess. She had a series of damaging romantic relationships and she abused alcohol, marijuana, opium, and, eventually, heroin. In 1947, she checked herself into a clinic for treatment of her addictions. Within a few weeks of her discharge she was arrested for drug possession, and she served nine and a half months at a federal detention center in Virginia. Ten days after her release, she made a triumphant return to a packed Carnegie Hall, but her career was in trouble. Because of her conviction, she lost her license to perform in nightclubs in New York City. She continued to tour and record, but years of substance abuse had taken their toll on her body and her voice.

Considered by many to be the greatest jazz singer ever recorded, Holiday will always be remembered for her interpretive gift, which continues to influence and inspire performers and listeners alike.

Katharine Hepburn
actor (1909–)

"I've just done what I damn well wanted to," declared the fiercely independent Katharine Hepburn. This philosophy has served her well; defying convention, she spoke her mind, always wore pants, and carried on a twenty-seven-year-long romance with a married man. Nominated for more Oscars (twelve) than any other person, and winner of the most best actress Oscars (four), the legendary Hepburn created dozens of spirited characters full of intelligence, wit, and spunk.

Hepburn enjoyed a privileged and progressive upbringing in Fenwick, Connecticut. After graduating from Bryn Mawr College in 1928, she headed straight to New York City to become a star. Early in her career, Hepburn was fired from numerous acting

Below: Katharine Hepburn in *Woman of the Year*, her first pairing with longtime love Spencer Tracy.
Opposite: Billie Holiday in 1956.

ONE OF A KIND

jobs. "When I started out," she said, "I didn't have any desire to be an actress or to learn how to act, I just wanted to be famous."

Hepburn's performance in the Broadway play *The Warrior's Husband* in 1932 led to a film contract with RKO Studios. Her first film, *A Bill of Divorcement*, opposite John Barrymore, was a big hit. She appeared in a burst of films, including *Little Women*, *Christopher Strong*, and, in 1933, *Morning Glory*, for which she won the Academy Award for best actress. Just as quickly, her star faded when a couple of flops in the mid-1930s caused her to be labeled "box office poison" by theater owners. Hepburn returned to Broadway to stage her comeback. "That's when I learned to do only material I liked," she said. "When I did what other people told me to do, my career took a total nosedive. I learned to please myself because then, at least, I was pleasing someone."

With the influence of her millionaire boyfriend Howard Hughes, Hepburn bought the rights to *The Philadelphia Story* and had it rewritten to showcase her aristocratic style and sharp wit. A smash on Broadway, Hepburn triumphantly returned to Hollywood to make the film version.

Hepburn's fateful pairing with the versatile Spencer Tracy in *Woman of the Year* in 1942 created one of Hollywood's most enduring on- and off-screen romances. Though Tracy never divorced his estranged wife, he lived with Hepburn for twenty-seven years until his death in 1967. "I loved him and made a life for him that was irresistible to him," she wrote in her 1991 memoir, *Me: Stories of My Life*. "Otherwise, I think he would have wandered off." They made nine popular films together, including *Adam's Rib*, *Pat and Mike*, and *Desk Set*, and Tracy's last film, *Guess Who's Coming to Dinner*, in 1967, for which Hepburn earned her second Academy Award. The next year, at the age of fifty-nine, she won an unprecedented third best actress Oscar for her performance in *The Lion in Winter*. Other notable Hepburn films are *The African Queen* (1951), *Suddenly, Last Summer* (1959), *Long Day's Journey Into Night* (1962), and *On Golden Pond* (1981), for which she won a fourth Oscar.

"I look back and think, my God, I was lucky," she said at eighty-four years old. "I think I was born at the right time for the thing I turned into, this new kind of modern woman who wanted to wear pants, wanted to live like a man. I know how lucky I was."

Eva Perón
first lady (1919–1952)

Born out of wedlock and into poverty, scrappy Eva Perón rose to the heights of political power in Argentina before she was thirty years old. Married to Colonel Juan Perón, a military strongman twice her age, she orchestrated his ascension to the presidency. Drawing on her background as a radio and film actor, Perón, called Evita by her fans, carefully staged dramatic appeals to the poor, to women, and to union workers, fanatically touting her husband as the answer to their oppression. "Without fanaticism, one cannot accomplish anything," she claimed. In 1946, Juan Perón won easily and their paradoxical reign began.

Evita Perón did much for her people, the *descamisados* (the shirtless ones), while satisfying her own appetite for power.

Above: Eva Perón in 1945. **Opposite:** Katharine Hepburn.

Outraged by the conditions of the poor, she established the Eva Perón Foundation, which soon was receiving twelve thousand petitions for help each day. To annoy her critics (primarily military government officials who were offended by her class background and gender) and to flaunt her position, Evita invited the petitioners to visit her personally. She was as warm and genuine when she granted an audience to poor people as she was cold and ruthless in censoring politicians and media who dared to fault her. She also skimmed large sums of money from the foundation for her own personal pleasures.

Largely credited with winning women the right to vote in 1947, Evita then rallied thousands of women to join the Perónist Women's Party by speaking passionately about the inequities suffered by working women, although her solution was less than empowering. "To be a Perónist is, for a woman, to be loyal and to have blind confidence in Perón," she exulted. While constantly professing her own blind faith in Perón, Evita in fact shaped many of his policies and ardently promoted them in Argentina and Europe. She captivated the world with her naked ambition, youth, and glamour. Perón lived in her shadow.

In 1951, Evita was stricken suddenly with uterine cancer, but she refused to accept the diagnosis or treatment. Referring to her critics, she said, "All of them want me out of politics. They won't succeed." Forced by her husband to spend time relaxing at their weekend retreat, Evita was restless and spent much of her time on the telephone. Perón ordered the wires cut, but Evita had them reconnected and covered her telephone with a pillow so that he wouldn't hear it ring.

Although Evita was quite sick, a populist movement to draft her to run for the vice presidency emerged. Without directly addressing her possible candidacy, she obliquely encouraged a crowd of more than one million in August of 1951. "I shall always do what the people wish," she said. "But I tell you, just as I said five years ago, that I would rather be Evita than the wife of the President, if this Evita could do anything for the pain of my country." In the end, her husband decided that she would not run. Evita died the following year, at the age of thirty-three, leaving behind a country in mourning and a legacy that still inspires controversy.

Julia Child
chef (1912–)

*A*aving dropped a potato pancake on the counter on live television, celebrated chef Julia Child didn't miss a beat. Tossing it back into the pan, she happily reassured her viewers, "Remember, you're all alone in the kitchen and no one can see you." As the French Chef on public television, with her imposing six-foot-two (185 cm) frame, distinctive high-pitched warble, and hilariously down-home style, she literally tackled *haute cuisine* and became an overnight sensation. Child introduced French cuisine to the American public and demystified the art of gourmet cooking through wildly popular cookbooks and television programs.

Above: Culinary wonder Julia Child in her kitchen. **Opposite:** Toni Morrison, whose evocative fiction has earned her a Pulitzer Prize and a Nobel Prize, in 1985.

Originally from Pasadena, California, Julia McWilliams graduated from Smith College in 1934. With the outbreak of World War II, she joined the Office of Strategic Services with the romantic notion that she would become a spy. Instead she was made a file clerk in Washington, D.C., and then in Ceylon, where she met and married Foreign Service officer Paul Cushing Child in 1946. Two years later, the Childs were stationed in France, and Julia had her first taste of French food. "I wasn't just in love," she has said of this culinary experience, "I was in hysterics for about five years."

Like many Americans, Child was intimidated by French cuisine. She took classes at the world-renowned Cordon Bleu cooking school, where she met gourmets Simone Beck and Louisette Bertholle. Together they opened their own school, called L'Ecole des Trois Gourmandes, and several years later collaborated on the book *Mastering the Art of French Cooking*, which *The New York Times* hailed as a masterpiece. Still considered the definitive English-language book on traditional French cuisine, it introduced classic French dishes to Americans cooking at home.

On a promotional tour for the book after moving back to the United States, Child was interviewed on Boston's public television station. The author brought along a copper bowl and whisk and whipped up an omelette on a hotplate before the startled host. The station immediately asked her to tape some pilot programs. *The French Chef* debuted on February 11, 1963. It was an instant hit and won an Emmy award. A natural performer, the jaunty Child mastered the art of chatting while executing complex culinary moves. Her warts-and-all shows were broadcast live, and she made mistakes, dropped food, and burned dishes with as much aplomb as she whipped a fillet of trout into a delicate mousse. "This is one of those nice messy dishes that you get all over you," she once said while gouging lobsters with gusto. "I like the process of cooking—I'm not interested in dishes that take three minutes and have no cholesterol."

Child appeared on television on and off for almost thirty years, continued to publish cookbooks, and wrote about cooking for magazines and newspapers. Still hard at work in her eighties, the upbeat Child has survived a radical mastectomy, hip replacement, and the death of her beloved husband. "In this line of work, you never have to retire," she explained. "You keep right on until you're through." She relishes life and dismisses critics who say her recipes are unhealthy. "I don't eat things because they are good for me," she said. "I eat things because they are good."

Toni Morrison
writer (1931 –)

A breathtaking novelist, Toni Morrison taps the mythic roots of African-American culture, tradition, and memory, rendering the specificity of individual lives within uniquely black contexts. Her novels encompass the breadth of African-American experience—the joys and sorrows, the passions and pain. She proudly describes herself as a black woman writer and said unapologetically, "I simply wanted to write literature that was irrevocably, indisputably Black, not because its characters were, or because I was, but because it took as its creative task and sought as its credentials those recognized and

verifiable principles of Black art." Universally lauded for her talent and artistry in creating sharply drawn, complex characters and authentic dialogue, Morrison is considered one of the world's greatest contemporary writers.

Morrison, who was born Chloe Anthony Wofford, grew up in Lorain, Ohio, in a family that celebrated black culture, art, and folklore and fostered a strong appreciation of black community. After earning an undergraduate degree in English at Howard University (where she started going by the name Toni) and a master's degree in English from Cornell University in 1955, she taught, first at Texas Southern University and then at Howard, from 1958 to 1964.

In 1957, she married architect Harold Morrison, with whom she had two sons. Divorced in 1964, she became a textbook editor for Random House in upstate New York. Within three years, she was a senior editor at Random House in New York City. There, and later as a literary critic, Morrison promoted and facilitated the works of other African-American writers. In 1974, she was responsible for the publication of *The Black Book*, a multifaceted portrayal of African-American history.

Black history and everyday life are background and foreground in her novels. *The Bluest Eye*, Morrison's stunning first novel, tells the devastating story of a young black girl named Pecola Breedlove. Constantly told that she is ugly, Pecola dreams of, and finally becomes obsessed with, having the blue eyes of a white girl; she ultimately escapes into madness. Morrison followed with *Sula*, *Song of Solomon*, *Tar Baby*, and *Beloved*, the powerful first novel in a trilogy for which she won the 1988 Pulitzer Prize for fiction. An unblinking portrayal of the horrors of slavery, *Beloved* is based on a true story of a woman who escaped slavery with her children and, facing imminent capture, tried to kill her children rather than see them re-enslaved. The second novel in the trilogy, *Jazz*, moves to the period of black migration to northern cities.

Morrison's body of work is as challenging as it is artistic, deftly posing profound questions, yet providing few easy answers. "I never played it safe in a book," she explains. "I never tried to play to the gallery. For me, it was this extraordinary exploration. You have to be willing to think the unthinkable."

When Morrison left her job at Random House in 1984, she was an established literary giant. In 1993, she became the first African-American woman to win the Nobel Prize in literature.

"I would like my work to do two things: be as demanding and sophisticated as I want it to be, and at the same time be accessible in a sort of emotional way to lots of people, just like jazz," she mused in a recent interview. "That's a hard task. But that's what I want to do."

Madonna
singer and actor (1958–)

*C*ourting controversy and fame, Madonna made herself into a phenomenally successful recording artist and performer while maintaining tight control of her career. With unapologetically naked ambition, she bared everything from

her midriff to her bustier to her entire body as she built an empire of hot dance singles, erotic music videos, world concert tours, and her own independent label. "How could I have been anything else but what I am, having been named Madonna?" she said. "I would either have ended up a nun or this."

One of eight children, she was born Madonna Ciccone near Detroit, Michigan; her mother died when Madonna was six. She earned a dance scholarship to the University of Michigan in 1976 but soon struck out for New York City with little money and big dreams. Although she quickly landed chorus line gigs with the Alvin Ailey and Martha Graham dance troupes, she wasn't content to remain in the background.

Working low-wage jobs by day, she sang at local dance clubs at night. In 1982, DJ Mark Kamins got her in the door at Warner Bros. Music, which released her self-titled album in 1983. The upbeat single "Holiday" danced its way from New York City clubs to urban radio stations to the top of *Billboard*'s pop chart, as did her next two singles, "Lucky Star" and "Borderline." *Like a Virgin* was released the following year; the title track became her first number-one hit. In 1985, Madonna sold more singles and albums than any other artist. Her unabashed sexuality, irresistible dance tunes, and provocative personal life catapulted her to the status of an American icon.

She debuted in the feature films *Vision Quest* and *Desperately Seeking Susan* and received accolades for her Broadway performance in David Mamet's *Speed-the-Plough*. Although she appeared in a number of movies, her film career never approached the heights of her musical achievements.

The title song of her 1989 album, *Like A Prayer*, and its risqué video (in which a scantily clad Madonna kisses a black saint and displays stigmata, representing the five wounds Jesus received on the cross) caused a huge scandal and proved that controversy sells. Madonna became the highest-grossing woman in the entertainment industry, with a net worth of about $70 million. Her next efforts—the Blonde Ambition tour, the documentary *Truth or Dare*, and the X-rated book *Sex*—were deliberately scandalous. "Sick and perverted always appeals to me," she said. With a new Warner Bros. seven-year contract worth $60 million, apparently, she isn't alone. Part of the deal included running her own label, Maverick,

Above: Madonna reveals herself at the 44th International Film Festival in Cannes. **Opposite:** Madonna performs "Sooner or Later," nominated for a best original song Oscar, at the 1991 Academy Awards.

which struck gold with Alanis Morissette's *Jagged Little Pill*, the best-selling album by a female artist in history.

Madonna played the role of her soul mate, Eva Perón, in the lavish 1996 film *Evita*, for which she won the Golden Globe award for best actress in a musical or comedy. That year, she also took on her most treasured role to date, giving birth to her daughter, Lourdes Maria Ciccone León. It's impossible to predict the next move for Madonna, who has said, "It's better to live one year as a tiger than hundred as a sheep."

6

TO TELL THE TRUTH

Huda Shaarawi, activist

Dorothea Lange, photographer

Gabriela Mistral, poet

Ann Landers, columnist

Rachel Carson, environmentalist

Maya Angelou, poet and writer

Yoshiko Uchida, writer

Helen Thomas, journalist

Barbara Jordan, politician

Lois Gibbs, environmentalist

Audre Lorde, poet and activist

Eka Esu-Williams, immunologist and AIDS educator

Anita Hill, law professor

Rigoberta Menchú, activist

Testifying to their own truths or helping others realize theirs, these women stood their ground and held fast to their visions. Unblinking and unwavering, their lives remind us that telling the simple truth is a compelling act of courage.

Helen Thomas

Ann Landers

Barbara Jordan

Anita Hill

Rachel Carson

Gabriela Mistral

Rigoberta Menchú

Eva Con-Williams

Maya Angelou

Huda Shaarawi
activist (1879–1947)

After attending a women's conference in Rome in 1923, Huda Shaarawi committed a revolutionary act at a packed train station in Cairo: she removed her veil. This public defiance of an age-old tradition stunned the crowd into silence. Then a few women who knew Shaarawi broke into applause and tore off their veils. This act of daring was not just a symbolic gesture for Shaarawi—she spent most of her life advocating for the independence of women as a leader of the Egyptian feminist movement.

At the age of twenty-one, Shaarawi was already coaxing women to take extraordinary personal risks to subvert the conventional patriarchal order. She organized lectures on women's status that for the first time brought women out of their homes and into public halls. She persuaded Egyptian princesses to establish a welfare fund for impoverished women. In 1919, she led the largest women's demonstration against British colonialism, persuading her followers to stand perfectly still for three hours in the blazing sun in silent protest.

Born into a family of privilege, Huda was educated at home by private tutors. Even as a child, she resented gender roles. "I once asked Umm Kariba [one of her father's wives] why everyone paid more attention to my brother than to me," she wrote in her book, *Harem Years: The Memoirs of an Egyptian Feminist*, "'Haven't you understood yet?' she asked gently...'you are a girl and he is a boy.'" The honor of an Egyptian man was based on the purity of the women in his household; therefore, women were kept in seclusion, venturing into public only in the company of a male relative or a eunuch, with their heads covered.

Huda was furious when she was betrothed at the age of thirteen as a second wife to a much older cousin, Ali Shaarawi. She entered the harem, but the marriage was troubled and she was able to live apart from her husband for seven years. They finally reconciled and had two children, but Shaarawi was already mobilizing women to fight for their rights. In 1910, she opened a school for girls that focused on academics rather than traditional female skills like midwifery.

The same year that she publicly removed her veil, Shaarawi helped found the Egyptian Feminist Union; she served as its president for twenty-four years. Under her forceful leadership, the union successfully lobbied for raising the minimum age of marriage for girls to sixteen, improving women's health care, and creating educational opportunities for women and girls—including the opening of Egypt's first secondary school for girls in 1927. "I observed how women without learning tremble with embarrassment and fright if called upon to speak a few words to a man from behind a screen," she wrote. This observation "convinced me that, with learning, women could be the equals of men if not surpass them."

Dorothea Lange
photographer (1895–1965)

A young mother, pensive, burdened, her face strained with worry and hopelessness, peers from a tattered tent that houses her and her children. This photograph is an enduring image of the Great Depression, and it is part of the

TO TELL THE TRUTH

legacy of Dorothea Lange, a documentary photographer who chronicled some of the most poignant chapters in United States history.

Growing up on the Lower East Side of Manhattan, Dorothea, who walked with a pronounced limp from a bout with polio, felt alienated from her peers. She preferred wandering around New York City, observing its people and sights, to attending school. By the time she graduated from high school, she knew she wanted to be a photographer, though she had never owned a camera or even taken a picture.

While attending the New York Training School for Teachers, she became an apprentice photographer. She left New York in 1918 for San Francisco, where she married, had two children, and made an excellent living for several years running her own portrait studio, which served a well-to-do clientele. But as the Depression tightened its grip on the nation, Lange became increasingly disturbed by the sight of unemployed men in the street, and she felt compelled to document the devastating impact of this national tragedy on individuals. "It came to me," she said, "that what I had to do was to take pictures and concentrate upon people, only people, all kinds of people, people who paid me and people who didn't."

In 1934, she put together an exhibition of her work, which drew the attention of Paul S. Taylor, a social economist at the University of California. Lange and Taylor started working together for the California State Emergency Relief Administration to document the living conditions of workers in the state; within two years she divorced her husband and married Taylor. Hired by the Farm Security Administration to record the migration of farm people from the Dust Bowl of Oklahoma, she lived among the Okies, and her photographs captured their anguish and loss. The result was the 1939 book *An American Exodus: A Record of Human Erosion*, whose compelling images were influential in helping to secure federal relief funding for the migrant workers.

In 1942, the United States government, in the midst of World War II, ordered the internment of Japanese residents. When the War Relocation Authority hired Lange to make a photographic record of the internment, she gave up a Guggenheim fellowship to live among the families as they were removed from their homes. Lange was horrified by what she saw. Many of her heartbreaking photographs, clearly sympathetic to the Japanese experience, were impounded by the federal government until the war was over.

In her later career, Lange became fascinated by "the familiar," by the images of everyday life. She focused primarily on her own home and family, occasionally taking some assignments for *Life* magazine. Her legacy of pictures that speak volumes about the human experience raised the consciousness of a nation.

Opposite: In this 1936 signature photograph, Dorothea Lange captures the despair wrought by the Great Depression.
Below: Gabriela Mistral in 1945.

Gabriela Mistral
poet (1889–1957)

*a*lthough Gabriela Mistral went to school for only three years, it was time enough to discover her love of poetry. Growing up in poverty in a Chilean village, she was inspired by the beautiful countryside and the surrounding Andes mountains. Her lush poetry often describes the natural terrain of

mistral, that blows down from the Alps for one hundred days each year. Her father deserted the family when she was three, leaving her mother struggling to provide for two daughters. Mistral's older sister, Emelina, taught Lucila at home and encouraged her to become a teacher as well. At age sixteen, Mistral got a job as an assistant teacher in La Cantera, where she fell in love with a railway worker. The relationship didn't last, but Mistral was devastated when the young man took his own life two years later. A postcard from her was the only item found on his body.

Mistral expressed her grief through poetry, in a collection called *Sonnets of Death*, which she didn't publish for several years. In 1912, she was teaching in a town near Santiago and began publishing her poetry in a variety of the city's periodicals. Soon she became well known in Chilean literary circles. In 1914, when she finally published three poems from *Sonnets of Death*, she won the national prize for poetry. Several years later, having also become a respected school administrator, Mistral was asked by the Mexican Minister of Education to create educational programs for the poor in his country. She established mobile libraries in Mexican rural communities and traveled to other countries to study effective methods of teaching. Mistral was committed to making literature accessible to all people, not just the elite.

The first published volume of Mistral's collected poems, *Desolación* (Desolation), published in 1922, explored her feelings about pain and death and garnered her an international reputation. Her next collection of poetry, *Ternura* (Tenderness), written for children, honors the joys of birth and motherhood. Later volumes include *Questions* (1930) and *Tala* (Havoc, 1938).

As Mistral's international popularity grew, she traveled extensively, representing her country at the League of Nations, the United Nations, and Chilean consulates around the world. She eventually settled in the United States, teaching at Columbia University, Barnard College, and Middlebury College. Mistral's later poems were more explicitly political, advocating for the rights of women, children, and indigenous people; she also wrote antifascist poems in response to the Spanish Civil War. In 1945, this rural schoolteacher, whose poetry touched the hearts of people of all backgrounds, accepted the Nobel Prize on behalf of Latin America and the "poets of my race."

her homeland, as well as the emotional terrain of motherhood, childhood, love, and love's betrayals. Mistral was awarded the Nobel Prize for poetry, becoming the first Latin American to be so honored.

Born Lucila Godoy Alcayaga, Mistral chose her pen name from the archangel Gabriel and the dry, cold wind, called the

Ann Landers

columnist (1918–)

*T*he naked truth is always better than the best-dressed lie" is typical of the no-nonsense advice given by Esther Pauline Friedman (a.k.a. Ann Landers), called Eppie by her friends and colleagues. She and her twin sister, Pauline Esther, were born in Sioux City, Iowa, on July 4, 1918. The sisters were married in a double ceremony in 1939; Eppie married Jules Lederer, who later made his fortune by starting Budget Rent-a-Car.

For many years, the couple lived in Wisconsin, where Eppie Lederer worked enthusiastically for the Democratic party, becoming influential and well-connected. In 1955, just after the Lederers had moved to Chicago, she entered a contest to replace Ruth Crowley, who wrote an advice column under the pen name Ann Landers for *The Chicago Sun-Times*. Asked to respond to several problems of hypothetical readers, Lederer thoroughly

Below: Ann Landers in 1982.

researched each question, consulting her high-powered friends (including a Supreme Court justice and the president of Notre Dame University) for their expertise—a technique that she would use consistently throughout her career.

She won the competition hands down. Her first column, which ran on October 16, 1955, featured other trademarks: common-sense advice, smart insights, and pithy, clever rejoinders. "Time wounds all heels," she wrote to a cheating husband. "You'll get yours." Within months of Eppie's becoming Ann Landers, her twin sister Pauline had become Abigail Van Buren, Dear Abby of the *San Francisco Chronicle*.

Ann Landers is now the most widely syndicated columnist in the world, reaching 90 million readers in more than twelve hundred newspapers. The two thousand letters she receives each day cover every conceivable human foible, drama, dilemma, and tragedy. She has been called upon to proffer wisdom on an amazing range of issues, from alcoholism, incest, and AIDS to bad breath, how to hang toilet paper (a controversy that elicited some fifteen thousand letters), and the gamut of troubled family relationships.

Readers appreciate not only Ann Landers' down-to-earth style but also her ability to adapt and change with the times. "The changes I have seen would twirl your turban," she once acknowledged. In 1972, she wrote, "I no longer believe that marriage means forever no matter how lousy it is—or for the sake of the children." (She and Lederer divorced after thirty-six years.) In 1981: "When I first got into this work, I thought a woman should remain a virgin until she married or died, whichever came first.... Well, I changed my mind about that." Occasionally, Landers makes the wrong call, and when she does, she is quick to it, self-administering "40 lashes with a wet noodle."

Some of her most memorable sayings are "The real trick is to stay alive as long as you live"; "Marriage is not a reform school"; "The best things in life aren't things;" and "Wake up and smell the coffee," which became the title of her sixth book.

Ann Landers was named the most influential woman in the United States in a 1978 *World Almanac* poll. Indeed, in more than four decades of doling out intelligent, plainspoken guidance, she has become one of the most trusted arbiters of American values.

TO TELL THE TRUTH

Rachel Carson
environmentalist (1907–1964)

The modern environmental protection movement has its roots in one woman's love of nature and her extraordinary gift of communicating the beauty and importance of the natural world to the general public. Rachel Carson dreamed of becoming a writer, majoring in English at the Pennsylvania College for Women. But she became fascinated by biology after taking a required course in the subject, and switched her major. She went on to earn a master's degree in zoology from Johns Hopkins University in 1932. "Biology has given me something to write about," she told a friend. "I will try in my writing to make animals in the woods and waters where they live as alive and as meaningful to others as they are to me."

In 1937, while working as an aquatic biologist with the U.S. Bureau of Fisheries, Carson did just that. She published a beautifully written article in *Atlantic Monthly* called "Undersea," which she eventually developed into a critically acclaimed book, *Under the Sea Wind*.

In the meantime, Carson's older sister died, leaving two young daughters for Carson and her mother to raise. With a family to support, she continued working for what was now the Fish and Wildlife Service, and by 1949, she was editor-in-chief of all of its publications. Over several years, in her very limited spare time, Carson wrote her second book, *The Sea Around Us*. Published in 1951, it became an immediate bestseller, appreciated by readers and critics alike for its eloquent, beautiful portrayal of the ocean's complex and surprising ecosystem.

The success of *The Sea Around Us* enabled Carson to leave the Fish and Wildlife Service to devote herself to writing full time. She built a summer cottage on the coast of Maine, where she wrote her follow-up book, *The Edge of the Sea*.

Above: Rachel Carson in 1951. **Opposite:** Rachel Carson, who combined her loves of writing and nature, looking through a microscope.

By 1958, Carson had long been concerned about the unregulated and indiscriminate use of DDT and other chemical pesticides and herbicides, which had become widespread after World War II. At the urging of a friend whose Massachusetts bird sanctuary had been decimated after the area was sprayed with DDT, Carson embarked on years of research into the deadly impact of toxic chemicals on the earth, air, and water. The result was *Silent Spring*, whose tone was distinctly different from that of her other books. In this prescient work, Carson sounded a note of alarm: "For the first time in the history of the world, every human being is now subject to contact with dangerous chemicals, from the moment of conception until death."

Silent Spring created a new awareness of ecology, mobilized citizens against the poisoning of the environment, and challenged corporate irresponsibility. As a result, Carson was vilified by pesticide companies even as she was lauded by scientists, critics, and her readers. But her research stood up to scrutiny, and as a direct result of her work, President John F. Kennedy ordered a government panel to study the environmental impact of pesticides.

While she was writing *Silent Spring*, Carson was battling bone cancer. She lived until 1964, long enough to testify before Congress for environmental legislation and to see the launching of a new ecology movement that was inspired by her work.

Maya Angelou
poet and writer (1928–)

Swaying to the rhythm of her own powerful voice, Renaissance woman Maya Angelou recited her poem "On the Pulse of Morning" to a rapt worldwide audience at the inauguration of Bill Clinton in January 1993. Angelou's stirring performance created such a tremendous demand for her writing that her classic 1970 autobiography, *I Know Why the Caged Bird Sings*, has since become the longest-running nonfiction paperback by an African American on the *New York Times* bestseller list. Hers is an extraordinary journey from mute child to one of the most eloquent orators of our time.

Born Marguerite Johnson, she was given the nickname "Maya" by her brother. Maya's parents divorced when she was quite young; she and her brother were raised in Stamps, Arkansas, by their paternal grandmother, Annie Henderson. While visiting her mother in St. Louis, seven-year-old Maya was raped by her mother's boyfriend. The man was convicted and later beaten to death in jail. Feeling responsible for his death, she vowed not to speak in public again. Maya's self-imposed silence lasted for five years, and she was ostracized by most of the people in Stamps. But, she remembers, her grandmother stood by her, frequently saying, "Sister, Mama don't care what these people say about you being a moron, being an idiot. Mama don't care. Mama know, Sister, when you and the good Lord get ready, you're gonna be a preacher." With her grandmother's love and the encouragement of a teacher who introduced her to literature, Maya graduated from the eighth grade first in her class.

Since then, her creative expression has taken on myriad forms. Starting out as an actor and dancer in New York, having taken the name Angelou, she won a featured role in a traveling production of George Gershwin's opera *Porgy and Bess*, touring twenty-two countries in Europe and Africa. In 1961, she performed alongside Louis Gossett Jr., James Earl Jones, and Cicely Tyson in an acclaimed off-Broadway production of Jean Genet's *The Blacks*.

By 1961, Angelou was also establishing her reputation as a writer of poetry, short stories, and songs. That same year, she moved to Cairo with South African activist Vusumzi Make and her teenage son, Guy, to whom she had given birth at the age of sixteen. After working as an associate editor for the *Arab Observer*, she left Make and moved with her son to Ghana, where he attended university and she made her living as a journalist. Returning to the United States, Angelou wrote a ten-part television series, *Black, Blues, Black* (1968), exploring the impact of African culture on American life. Shortly thereafter, she wrote her first book, *I Know Why the Caged Bird Sings*, which was nominated for a National Book Award. In 1971, her collection of poems *Just Give Me a Cool Drink of Water 'fore I Diiie* was nominated for a Pulitzer Prize.

Now fluent in six languages, the once-mute Angelou has amassed an impressive and still-growing body of work that includes volumes of poetry, essays, children's books, autobiographies, plays, screenplays, and performances. She has been awarded more than fifty honorary degrees. Angelou's recent best-selling essay collection is aptly titled *Wouldn't Take Nothing for My Journey Now*.

Opposite: Maya Angelou envisions a hopeful future in the poem she created for the 1993 inauguration of Bill Clinton.
Below: Children's-book author Yoshiko Uchida.

Yoshiko Uchida
writer (1920–1992)

Children's book author Yoshiko Uchida's celebrated career had a humble beginning: she wrote her first book on brown wrapping paper at the age of ten. Since then, Uchida single-handedly created the genre of Japanese-American children's literature, writing more than twenty-five books that explored issues of cultural pride, immigration, and racism through the eyes of her young characters.

As a child growing up in Berkeley, California, in the 1930s, Uchida found virtually no children's books featuring Asian families. Drawing on her own experiences as a child of Japanese immigrants, she dedicated her entire career to telling the rich stories of her people. "I hope to give to young Asians a sense of their history," she said. "At the same time, I want to dispel the stereotypic image still held by many non-Asians about the Japanese Americans and write about them as real people. I hope to convey as well the strength of spirit and the sense of hope and purpose I have seen in many first-generation Japanese Americans."

Uchida and her family were among the more than 120,000 people of Japanese ancestry (two-thirds of them U.S. citizens) forced from their homes and interned by presidential order after the bombing of Pearl Harbor. She was held captive throughout the war years, first temporarily at San Bruno's Tanforan race track, where she received her diploma from the University of California at Berkeley in the horse stall where she and her family were staying, and then at Topaz, an internment camp in the bleak Utah desert. Uchida told her painful story to children through the clear eyes of her eleven-year-old character, Yuki, in *Journey to Topaz* (1971) and *Journey Home* (1978). Uchida personally visited countless classrooms, libraries, and bookstores throughout her life, discussing her ordeal so that children would know the truth about this shameful chapter in U.S. history.

After earning a graduate degree in education from Smith College, Uchida briefly worked as a secretary and a teacher before publishing her first children's book, *The Dancing Kettle and Other Japanese Folk Tales*, in 1949, based on the folk tales she had heard as a child. Later, a Ford Foundation fellowship took her to Japan to collect additional stories. While in Japan, she wrote extensively about craftspeople and even studied weaving and pottery herself. Returning to California, she wrote for the magazine *Craft Horizons* before devoting herself to writing children's books full-time.

Writing well before the multicultural education movement took root, Uchida created characters that appeal to children of all

backgrounds by evoking universal childhood feelings. "But I hope my books will also enlarge and enrich the reader's understanding of the human condition," she wrote, "for I feel we must not only take pride in our special heritage, we must also strive to understand each other and to celebrate our common humanity."

Helen Thomas
journalist (1920–)

The daughter of Lebanese immigrants who could neither read nor write English, Helen Thomas grew up to become a pioneering newspaperwoman and the dean of the White House press corps.

Even as a girl, Helen was exhilarated by journalism; she joined the school newspaper at her public high school in Detroit and decided this would be her life's work. After graduating in 1942 from Wayne State University in Michigan, where she worked on the campus paper, Thomas moved to Washington, D.C., and got a job as a copy girl at the now-defunct *Washington Daily News*.

In 1943, Thomas began a tenure with United Press International (UPI) that has lasted more than half a century. She started out writing copy for radio, moving on to cover various federal government departments for the wire service. In 1960, Thomas got herself assigned to cover the Palm Springs family vacation of President-elect John F. Kennedy. She saw this as her "foot in the door" to White House journalism, a door that she then barged through, never to go back. She became a regular at presidential press conferences, soon gaining a reputation for tough, pointed questions, hard work, and dogged reporting. She was and still is known for being the first journalist to arrive at the White House press room in the morning and the last one to leave at night.

Though Thomas earned the respect and admiration of fellow reporters as well as the presidents she covered, some people wondered whether her extreme directness bordered on rudeness. "I don't think a tough question is disrespectful," she once explained. "I say, 'Mr. President.' I say, 'Thank you.' What else do you want?"

Below: The dramatic cover of Yoshiko Uchida's powerful children's story, *Journey to Topaz*, about the U.S. internment of Japanese Americans. **Opposite:** Helen Thomas in 1959.

JOURNEY TO TOPAZ

By Yoshiko Uchida

TO TELL THE TRUTH

Promoted in 1974 to UPI White House bureau chief, Thomas has covered eight presidents—Kennedy, Johnson, Nixon, Ford, Carter, Reagan, Bush, and Clinton. She is witness, watchdog, chronicler, and one of the most trusted voices in American journalism.

Barbara Jordan
politician (1936–1996)

Above: Helen Thomas in a social moment with the Gores and President Clinton at a Gridiron Club dinner.

*a*s she cast her vote to impeach the president of the United States, Congresswoman Barbara Jordan said, "My faith in the Constitution is whole, it is complete, it is total." A freshman member of the House Judiciary Committee, Jordan gave a nationally televised speech calling for the impeachment of President Richard Nixon that dramatically outlined the constitutional violations—which she called "high crimes and misdemeanors"—committed by his administration during the Watergate scandal and catapulted Jordan into the national spotlight. Although she acknowledged that when the Constitution was written, the phrase "We the people" did not include her as a black person and a woman, she fought hard to salvage her government's reputation through due process. "I am not going to sit here," she thundered, "and be an idle spectator to the diminution, the subversion, the destruction of the Constitution." A uniquely gifted orator, a meticulously prepared legislator, and a person of unassailable integrity, Jordan crafted a remarkable career as a public servant.

The youngest of three daughters born to a Baptist minister and a domestic worker in Houston, Texas, Jordan was especially close to her maternal grandfather. He fostered independence and excellence in young Barbara, who was a top-notch student and a silver-tongued debater. She majored in government at Texas Southern University and was on the debate team that tied with Harvard University—one of the proudest moments of her youth. She earned a law degree from Boston University (one of only two women in her class) and returned to Texas in 1959 to set up her private practice.

Working long hours providing legal assistance to the poor, Jordan decided that she could extend her effectiveness by serving

During the Watergate scandal, Thomas broke a number of exclusive stories. She had gained the trust of Martha Mitchell, the wife of Attorney General John Mitchell, who later served time for his role in the Watergate break-in and cover-up. In a series of late-night phone conversations, Martha Mitchell confided her suspicions and tipped Thomas off to her insider observations.

In 1972, Thomas was the only print journalist to travel with Nixon on his breakthrough trip to China, and she can boast of many firsts, including being the first woman officer of the National Press Club; the first woman officer and first woman president of the White House Correspondents Association; and first woman member and first woman president of the Gridiron Club, the exclusive Washington journalists' group.

Above: Gifted orator Barbara Jordan electrifies the 1992 Democratic National Convention. **Below left:** Congresswoman Barbara Jordan in 1976.

in elected office. She lost twice in her bid for a seat in the state House of Representatives; then in 1966, she ran for the state Senate and won. Jordan was the first black Texan to be elected to the state legislature since 1883 and the first black woman in its history. Her near-meteoric rise to prominence in Texas politics can be attributed to carefully working the old-boy network. "If you're going to play the game properly, you'd better know every rule," she said. In 1972, she was elected to the U.S. House of Representatives. Known for her effectiveness, Jordan championed the rights of the disenfranchised, for example, sponsoring state legislation on workers' compensation and federal legislation to broaden the Voting Rights Act to cover Mexican Americans and other minorities.

But it was her skills as an orator that continued to bring Jordan accolades and opportunities. In 1976, as the first woman to deliver the keynote address at a Democratic convention, she

TO TELL THE TRUTH

ignited the American public with a fiery speech. Her name was frequently mentioned as a possible vice presidential candidate or Supreme Court nominee. After a disarmingly brief tenure in Congress, Jordan retired from public office in 1978 to teach at the Lyndon B. Johnson School of Public Affairs at the University of Texas.

"What the people want is very simple," she said. "They want an America as good as its promise." Jordan, through personal example and stellar leadership, devoted her life to moving the country closer to that ideal.

Lois Gibbs
environmentalist (1951 –)

*I*n the spring of 1978, Lois Gibbs, a shy homemaker in Niagara Falls, New York, read in a newspaper report that her son's elementary school was built atop a twenty-thousand-ton (18,140t) toxic chemical dump. The story outlined the dozens of chemicals that had been dumped in nearby Love Canal between 1920 and 1953 and described the various diseases that exposure to these chemicals could cause.

It was a crystallizing moment for Gibbs, whose son had suffered from ailments that included pneumonia, epilepsy, asthma, and a liver disorder, and whose three-year-old daughter had a rare, life-threatening blood disease. Gibbs had been told that her children were just sickly; now she realized that there was a more sinister reason for her family's anguish. Thus began her transformation into a gutsy, combative, controversial environmental activist.

After failing to get her son transferred, Gibbs wrote up a petition that asked the school board to close the school and, summoning all of her courage, started knocking on doors. Her neighbors shared alarming stories of miscarriages, birth defects, cancers, and mysterious illnesses. "They were all in the same state I was in," she recalled. "I realized this is not about the school. This is about the whole neighborhood."

By August, Gibbs and her neighbor Debbie Cerrillo presented their case and the petition to the New York state health commissioner, who ordered the closing of the school and the evacuation of 239 families who lived in the immediate vicinity of the site. Yet hundreds of people living in a ten-square-block area just outside the evacuation zone, including the Gibbs and Cerrillo families, were told that they were not at risk.

Outraged, the remaining residents organized the Love Canal Homeowners Association (LCHA), which mobilized the working-class neighborhood, demanding that the government relocate them. Gibbs led the group in highly visible, often controversial protests. Members marched in the streets on Mother's Day, carried symbolic coffins to the state capitol, held prayer vigils, and once held two Environmental Protection Agency officials hostage for five hours. They hounded Governor Hugh Carey and President Jimmy Carter. Gibbs's children appeared at protests with signs reading "How Long Will I Live?"

The LCHA completed a health survey in February 1979 that showed extremely high incidences of deaths, birth defects, and diseases, and that out of twenty-two pregnancies occurring among Love Canal women, only four healthy babies were born. When officials dismissed the survey results, the group stepped up its efforts, making Love Canal a

Audre Lorde
poet and activist (1934–1992)

Above: Visionary poet and writer Audre Lorde. **Opposite:** Gibbs meets the press after her organization released two Environmental Protection Agency officials who were held hostage for five hours.

*A*udre Lorde's life and words are a guiding light to feminists, lesbians, black women and men, and anyone who cares about fighting oppression.

As a poet and an essayist, Lorde offered searingly honest personal reflections intertwined with her broad, spirited political vision. "I speak without concern for the accusations / that I am too much or too little woman / that I am too Black or too white / or too much myself..." she wrote in her 1971 poem "Prologue."

Lorde insisted on speaking from her full identity, which she named "Black, feminist, lesbian, poet, mother, warrior." As early as the 1970s, Lorde was rejecting the notion that there was a "hierarchy of oppression," pointing out that sexism, racism, homophobia, and class oppression are inseparable, and that anyone committed to ending one form of bigotry must learn to challenge all of them. Out of this vision, she worked to build bridges between the black, feminist, and lesbian and gay communities.

At the same time, Lorde warned white feminists not to gloss over women's very real differences. "Some problems we share as women, some we do not," she wrote. "You fear your children will grow up to join the patriarchy and testify against you; we fear our children will be dragged from a car and shot down in the street, and you will turn your backs upon the reasons they are dying."

Born during the Depression to West Indian immigrant parents, Lorde grew up in Harlem. Her book *Zami: A New Spelling of My Name*, which Lorde characterized as "biomythography," captured the gay Greenwich Village scene in which she came of age in the 1950s. After graduating from Hunter College and Columbia University School of Library Science, she became a hugely popular English professor at Hunter. Lorde wrote five volumes of prose and eight collections of poetry; in 1991, she was named poet laureate of New York state. Lorde was also a co-founder of Kitchen Table: Women of Color Press, the United States's first publisher specializing in books by women of color; and of Sisterhood in Support of Sisters in South Africa, which raises money for South African women's self-help groups.

household term. In October 1980, President Carter finally ordered the evacuation of nine hundred families.

Gibbs moved to Washington, D.C., and founded Citizens' Clearinghouse for Hazardous Waste to provide direct assistance to people who are living in hazardous environments. One of her campaigns has been an effort to block the proposed resettling of Love Canal. She has had two more children with her second husband; her older son and daughter, now in their twenties, have lingering health problems.

"How did I make the leap from caring for my children to caring for all children?" she asked. "I was so angry at what they did to my life that I hold a grudge. And that helped me make the leap."

A visionary proponent of the value of diversity, Lorde wrote in *Sister/Outsider*, a book of her essays and speeches, "Now we must recognize differences among women who are our equals, neither inferior nor superior, and devise ways to use each other's differences to enrich our visions and our joint struggles."

In 1978, Lorde was diagnosed with breast cancer, which later spread to her liver. She faced the disease surrounded by her family—her life partner, Frances Clayton, and Lorde's son and daughter, whom they raised together. Characteristically, she wrote and spoke out about her personal thoughts and fears, as well as her rage about the treatment of breast cancer patients by the medical establishment. Published in 1980, *The Cancer Journals* helped to heal survivors, raise consciousness, and intensify feminist activism on breast cancer.

Eka Esu-Williams
immunologist and AIDS educator (1950–)

In the battle against HIV/AIDS, immunologist Eka Esu-Williams is facing more than a worldwide epidemic. As the president of the Society for Women Against AIDS in Africa (SWAA), she is also working hard to help women overcome the devastating impact of tradition, sexism, and poverty on the struggle to prevent the spread of this disease. For many people, especially women in developing countries, she says, "surviving the era of AIDS will hinge on our own personal power." An internationally respected expert, Esu-Williams is an urgent and eloquent voice for women with HIV/AIDS.

Raised in a large family in northern Nigeria, Esu-Williams is the daughter of a midwife and a father who believed strongly in the importance of education for girls. After earning a degree from the University of Nigeria, she studied immunology in Great Britain. She returned home in 1985 and began teaching at the University of Calabar, where she is now a senior lecturer in the Department of Immunology.

In 1988, when Esu-Williams founded SWAA, eighty percent of women who had AIDS were in Africa. Women are the fastest-growing population to be infected with the disease; World Health Organization experts predict that more women than men

Above: Immunologist Eka Esu-Williams educates everyone in her path—from the community platform to the global stage—about the prevention of HIV/AIDS. **Opposite:** Anita Hill enjoys a rare moment of levity as she testifies before the Senate Judiciary Committee.

will be infected with HIV by the year 2000. SWAA empowers African women by educating them about how HIV is transmitted, how to protect themselves from contracting AIDS, and how to talk to members of their families and their communities about AIDS. Esu-Williams takes this message to the international community, speaking out at world conferences and in the media.

Esu-Williams also provides direct community services as AIDS program coordinator for the state of Cross River, population two million. "Working with communities is an incredibly rewarding experience," she wrote, "especially when you see people becoming empowered through understanding." She lobbies hard for comprehensive and officially mandated sex education in schools, improved health services for women, and job training and education so that more women can avoid prostitution as their only employment option. "Strategies for controlling HIV require careful thought and planning, and," she wrote, "they must be sanctioned and supported by government as well as communities."

Thoughtful, confident, and dedicated, Esu-Williams is enlisting everyone she can to stop the spread of HIV/AIDS and knows that men as well as women must initiate and adopt HIV prevention efforts. "Modifying male attitudes about HIV and sexual behaviour is one of the significant factors in controlling this epidemic, and this constitutes a great challenge," she acknowledged. Esu-Williams is determined: "Our future is at stake."

Anita Hill
law professor (1956–)

n the fall of 1991, an intensely private law professor named Anita Hill testified before the U.S. Senate Judiciary Committee in televised hearings watched by more than forty million Americans. Her explosive testimony about the actions of Supreme Court nominee Clarence Thomas blew the lid off the conspiracy of silence that has surrounded sexual harassment and inspired thousands of women to come forward and tell the truth about their experiences. Although the names Hill and Thomas will always be inextricably linked, their stories were fundamentally irreconcilable, and much of the nation took sides.

Hill was a reluctant witness, pressured by senatorial aides to testify before the committee. On October 11, 1991, the nation sat transfixed as this poised black woman calmly faced an all-white panel of wealthy, powerful men and stated with unshakable resoluteness that Thomas, who had been her boss at the Equal Employment Opportunity Commission (EEOC), asked her out on dates, instigated sexually explicit conversations, vividly described scenarios from pornographic films, and bragged about his own sexual prowess. Members of the committee floundered in the face of her composure; in questioning Hill, their responses ranged from incredulity to hostility to buffoonery. Thomas vehemently denied her accusations, calling the Senate committee's

The impact of Hill's personal courage continues to be felt. Within a year after the hearings, the number of women filing charges of sexual harassment with the EEOC had increased by fifty percent. In 1992, women ran for and won a record number of elected offices—including four Senate seats—often mentioning Hill's ordeal as a factor in their decision to run. Today, most major employers have explicit written policies forbidding sexual harassment and outlining procedures for filing a complaint.

In her 1997 memoir, *Speaking Truth to Power*, Hill recounted her extraordinary journey from her family's peanut farm in rural Oklahoma, to the prestigious Yale Law School, to her years in the federal government, to her successful career as a law professor in her home state, and, finally, into the blinding spotlight of the Thomas hearings. Hill currently spends her days lecturing on women's issues, writing on sexual harassment, and encouraging women to speak out. "We need to turn the question around to look at the harasser, not the target," Hill said. "We need to be sure that we can go out and look anyone who is a victim of harassment in the eye and say, 'You do not have to remain silent anymore.'"

Above: In the aftermath of the hearings, Anita Hill (left, with Gloria Steinem) continues to speak out against sexual harassment. **Opposite:** Nobel Peace Prize winner Rigoberta Menchú fights for the rights of indigenous peoples.

actions "a high-tech lynching." For the next three days, a parade of character witnesses weighed in on Hill's charges as the public debate intensified. Many men were bewildered by the rage this case elicited in the women in their lives; women furiously accused men of "just not getting it."

Although legal scholars and some experts testified that Thomas was not qualified to be on the Supreme Court based solely on his judicial record, this aspect was lost in the firestorm of controversy surrounding Hill's accusations and intense pressure from the White House to confirm Thomas. On October 16, 1991, by a vote of fifty-two to forty-eight, the Senate confirmed Thomas as an associate justice of the Supreme Court.

Rigoberta Menchú
activist (1959–)

When Indian rights activist Rigoberta Menchú, fearing for her life, fled her homeland of Guatemala in 1981, she had no idea that she would one day become the world's best-known advocate for indigenous peoples. In her 1983 memoir, *I...Rigoberta Menchú*, she chronicled her heartbreaking story as a member of the desperately poor, illiterate, and despised indigenous majority, bringing the thirty-year conflict between the Indians and the Guatemalan military to the attention of the international community. In 1992, just days after the quincentennial celebration of the arrival of Christopher Columbus in the Americas, Menchú became the first indigenous person to win the Nobel Peace Prize.

When she was a child, Menchú's Quiché Indian family could not grow enough food to survive on their small plot of land, so they were forced to work as laborers on a coffee plantation. By the age of eight, Menchú had to leave school because she was working fifteen-hour days. The conditions on the plantation were so harsh that two of her brothers died. When the military-led government started seizing Indian land (in Guatemala, native people have no legal rights), Menchú's father, Vincente, became a leader in the peasant movement to reclaim the land. Menchú often accompanied her father on his travels, and together they founded the Committee for Peasant Unity. As a teenager, she realized that her father was often tricked in negotiations because he couldn't speak Spanish, so she taught herself the language—her fluency and eloquence took her foes by surprise.

As the Indian land-rights movement gained momentum, Menchú's father was jailed and her brother was captured, tortured, and then burned to death in a public square as Menchú and her mother watched. Her father was killed several months later, when the Spanish embassy that he and dozens of other Indian leaders were occupying was torched by the army. Her mother, a community leader and healer, was later kidnaped, raped, mutilated, and killed for demanding justice for her son's murder. Since the 1970s, an estimated 120,000 people have been killed in Guatemala's political violence; human rights groups accuse the military of responsibility for most of them. In 1981, wanted by the government, Menchú left Guatemala for Mexico.

Menchú frequently denounced the Guatemalan government for its widely documented human rights abuses and for murdering her family. In return, the government has accused her of being a left-wing militant belonging to the country's guerrilla movement—a charge she denies. Menchú has, however, written about using violence to defend their land. In 1993, she convened the second of two Summits of Indigenous Peoples, gathering leaders of native groups from five continents. She told them, "We say no to the peace that keeps us on our knees, no to the peace that keeps us in chains, no to the false peace that denies the values and contributions of our peoples."

With her $1.2 million Nobel Prize, Menchú set up a foundation in her father's name to aid indigenous peoples. "I would like to see Guatemala at peace, with indigenous and non-indigenous people living side by side," said Menchú. "I think it would be the most beautiful thing. Maybe I won't live to see it, but maybe others after me will."

POWER BROKERS

Mary Pickford, actor and businessperson

Ichikawa Fusae, suffragist and politician

Katharine Graham, newspaper publisher

Golda Meir, prime minister

Maggie Kuhn, activist

Nguyen Thi Binh, political activist

Billie Jean King, athlete

Barbara Walters, journalist

Margaret Thatcher, prime minister

Roseanne, actor and producer

Hanan Ashrawi, political leader

Oprah Winfrey, talk show host, actor, and producer

The few, the proud, the powerful. These women had—and have—real clout and the ability to use it. Often the only women in their professional circles, they rose to positions of influence through a combination of opportunity, chutzpah, and smarts.

Maggie Kuhn

Margaret Thatcher

Mary Pickford

Hanan Ashrawi

Katharine Graham

Golda Meir

Oprah Winfrey

Barbara Walters

Billie Jean King

Mary Pickford

actor and businessperson (1892–1979)

a s an actor, "America's Sweetheart" Mary Pickford appeared in almost two hundred films and was cherished by her millions of fans. As a savvy businesswoman, she made herself the most powerful woman in Hollywood.

Born Gladys Louise Smith in Toronto, Ontario, she started acting to help support her family after her father died. By the age of five, she was the main breadwinner, and at fifteen, she convinced legendary theater producer David Belasco (who renamed her Mary Pickford) to give her a shot on Broadway. She debuted in the play *The Warrens of Virginia* in 1907 and later joined a tour of the show.

The film industry at this time was new, fledgling, and not altogether respectable. But it paid better than stagework, so after a couple of years in the "legitimate" theater, Pickford went to work for the hugely powerful and pioneering filmmaker D.W. Griffith. Distinguished by her adorable, youthful appearance and her long mane of blonde curls, she was promoted as "Goldilocks" and "the Girl with the Curls," and between 1909 and 1910 she appeared in eighty-five silent shorts.

By 1914, Pickford was phenomenally popular; she had become the first film megastar. She received thousands of fan letters; she was mobbed at public appearances; her trademark hair was treated as a national treasure (even as late as 1928, when she bobbed her hair, it made the front page of *The New York Times*). No one had ever seen or experienced such extraordinary fame.

Pickford's film persona—an angelic but tough young girl who overcomes tragic circumstances through her virtue and pluckiness—was quickly and firmly established. Over the years, she was to play a wide range of roles, but her public always thought of her as an innocent, and well into her thirties she was playing girls.

Behind the scenes, Pickford was anything but a naive girl. She parlayed her popularity into real power, demanding and receiving pay equal to that of Charlie Chaplin. At her peak she was earning $350,000 a film, and she was the first person to become a millionaire from acting. She controlled her film projects and acted as director, even when someone else was credited. "Nobody ever directed me, not even Mr. Griffith," she said. "I respected him, yes...but when he told me to do things I didn't believe in, I wouldn't do them."

Realizing that film companies were making millions from her work, in 1919, Pickford, along with Griffith, Chaplin, businessman William S. Hart, and swashbuckling actor Douglas Fairbanks, formed their own studio, United Artists. But Pickford was careful to keep a low profile as a businesswoman, producer, and director, lest her adoring fans become disillusioned. "I am a servant of the public," she said. "I have never forgotten that." The following year, after ending a disastrous first marriage, Pickford married the dashing Fairbanks, and together they began their reign as America's favorite couple. Their famous Hollywood home, Pickfair, was known nationally as the country's "second White House."

Left: Mary Pickford emulates her more fashionable counterpart in *Rebecca of Sunnybrook Farm*, 1917. **Opposite:** Mary Pickford.

With the end of the silent film era, Pickford devoted herself to United Artists, where she served as its first vice president and produced several films, and became a philanthropist. She divorced Fairbanks in 1935 and two years later married actor Charles "Buddy" Rogers. Gradually she withdrew from public life. It would be decades before any woman even approached Pickford's level of power and influence in the film industry.

Ichikawa Fusae
suffragist and politician (1893–1981)

Suffragist Ichikawa Fusae in the year she was elected to the Japanese Diet (parliament), where she served for twenty-six years.

Growing up in a farming family in Japan, Ichikawa Fusae learned firsthand about hard work and the subjugation of women. As she watched her domineering father routinely batter her mother, she resolved to work to improve women's subservient status.

After working as a rural elementary school teacher, a stockbroker's clerk, a journalist, and a labor organizer, in 1919, Ichikawa helped found the New Women's Association, which successfully lobbied for the repeal of a law that prohibited women from attending political meetings.

In 1921, Ichikawa traveled to the United States, eager to work with and learn from American feminists, who had succeeded in winning women's right to vote just a year earlier. When she returned home in 1924, she joined the fledgling Japanese women's suffrage movement, co-founding the Woman Suffrage League of Japan.

For Ichikawa, women's suffrage was a logical and necessary component of democracy, in which she felt everyone should have a voice. As a woman who publicly championed not only the vote for women but the idea of women's fundamental equality, Ichikawa was fiercely attacked, enduring verbal and physical harassment from her opponents and ridicule from the press, which fixated on things like her smoking, wearing her hair short, and wearing Western-style clothes. "As long as you don't behave differently from other people, you escape criticism," she wrote. "But if you step up front and advocate some belief, you are bound to be criticized. In fact, one of the characteristics of a leader is that he is criticized."

The suffragists were unable to overcome intense resistance in the Japanese Diet (parliament), and as the country became preoccupied with World War II, their efforts seemed ever more futile. The Woman Suffrage League disbanded in 1940, and Ichikawa devoted her energies to improving conditions of women workers during the war. It was only after the war had ended and Japan was under Allied occupation that a women's suffrage bill was enacted.

In 1952, Ichikawa ran for public office in a low-budget, grassroots, independent campaign, winning a seat in the upper house of the Diet, which she held, with the exception of the years 1971 to 1974, until her death. In the Diet, she was known as a fierce fighter against corruption, making her as beloved in her years as a public official as she had been reviled as an activist.

Katharine Graham
newspaper publisher (1917–)

Katharine Graham never intended to be a media mogul. The fourth of five children of Eugene Meyer, a fabulously wealthy Wall Street financier, and Agnes Meyer, a well-connected socialite, she thought a woman's role in life was "to please a man, support him, marry him, have his children, and then bring them up…I certainly wasn't brought up to believe that women had a role in business." Nonetheless, Graham went on to become one of the most powerful figures in American politics and media.

Katharine Meyer grew up in an enormously privileged but emotionally distant family. After studying at Vassar College and the University of Chicago, she worked briefly as a reporter in San Francisco and then on the editorial page at *The Washington Post*, which her father had purchased in 1933. In 1940, she married Philip Graham, a charming, brilliant lawyer who a few years later became, in quick succession, associate publisher then publisher of the *Post*. In 1948, she and her husband bought the *Post* from her father for one dollar.

Philip Graham worked hard to build the company and increase profits. In 1954, he purchased the *Post's* main competitor, *The Times-Herald*, and later acquired *Newsweek* as well as several radio and television stations. He also took bold political stands and built connections with powerful national figures, including John F. Kennedy and Lyndon Johnson. Katharine Graham was busy managing their homes, hosting their social affairs, organizing their travels, raising their four children, and contributing to charity events, but she had no active role in the business.

All of that was to change dramatically and suddenly when Philip Graham, who had been suffering from manic depression, committed suicide in 1963. Graham took over as president of

135

Below: Katharine Graham in her office at *The Washington Post*, 1980. **Right:** Katharine Graham hobnobs with former President and Mrs. Jimmy Carter.

the Washington Post Company and, six years later, she also assumed the title of publisher.

Admittedly inexperienced, Graham made a lot of mistakes at first, for which she was sometimes viciously criticized, but she grew into the job. She eventually built the *Post* into a newspaper of international stature: investing in an expanded editorial staff; committing the paper to quality investigative reporting; and making tough decisions during tumultuous times.

In 1971, the *Post* and *The New York Times* courageously published extensive excerpts from the Pentagon Papers, the damning secret Defense Department account of the Vietnam War, and in the process elicited a crucial Supreme Court ruling against governmental prior restraint.

Under Graham's watch, reporters Carl Bernstein and Robert Woodward pursued the Watergate scandal relentlessly, following the trail of misconduct all the way to the Oval Office. In the face of threats, condemnation, and hostility from Nixon associates, Graham stood firmly behind her editors. The paper won a Pulitzer Prize; President Nixon resigned.

Nicknamed "Katharine the Great," she kept the paper going through the twenty-week strike by pressmen in 1973, often answering phones and taking classified ads herself. Her son became publisher in 1979, but Graham remained on as chairman and CEO until 1991.

Although Graham came to power, in her words, "by birth and by death," she took the reins with courage and grace, and her significant accomplishments are her own.

Golda Meir
prime minister (1898–1978)

One of Golda Meir's earliest memories was watching her father barricade the entrance to their home with wooden boards to protect the family from an anticipated pogrom. As a child in Kiev in the Ukraine, and later in Pinsk, Russia, Golda Mabovitch lived in terror of the violent, roving mobs who would attack Jewish homes and families. As an adult, she would devote her life to the establishment and nurturing of a sovereign Jewish state.

Above: Golda Meir in 1970. **Opposite:** Meir and adviser Daniel Lewin are in high spirits as a 1967 United Nations debate gets underway over the recommended withdrawal of Israel from the Gaza Strip.

At age eight, she moved with her family to Milwaukee, Wisconsin. When she was nineteen, Golda married house painter Morris Meyerson on the condition that he move with her to Palestine, where Zionists were encouraging Jews to settle on collective farms, claiming the land as they worked toward the establishment of a Jewish state. They lived on a kibbutz for two years, eventually settling in Jerusalem and having two children.

Golda Meyerson's life as a public official began in 1928, when she became secretary of the Women's Labor Council in Palestine's Jewish government-in-waiting. Shortly thereafter, she and her husband separated, and he returned to the United States. On May 14, 1948, the day the state of Israel was established, she was one of twenty-five people who signed the

Proclamation of Independence. On that same day, the Arab Legion declared war on the new country. Israel won its war of independence, and she became the minister of labor in the cabinet of the country's first prime minister, David Ben-Gurion, who suggested she take the Hebrew name Meir, which means "to illuminate." After seven years as labor minister, she was named foreign minister in 1956.

By 1968, a fatigued Meir had retired from government. But the following year, Prime Minister Levi Eshkol died, and the Labor Party called her back to serve out the remainder of his term. At the end of that time, to the surprise of many, she ran for and won a full four-year term.

During her years as prime minister, Israel's security was Meir's obsession. "As long as we live, our children and grandchildren...the state of Israel and Jewish life everywhere will be defended at all costs," she vowed. Although she often reiterated her willingness to meet at any time with Arab leaders, and did in fact negotiate with them for peace, she was criticized for being rigid and uncompromising, particularly in holding on to the territories—the West Bank, East Jerusalem, Sinai, the Gaza Strip, and the Golan Heights—that Israel had occupied since 1967. She fiercely defended her resolve, saying, "The world hates a Jew who hits back. The world loves us only when we are to be pitied."

In October of 1973, during the Jewish High Holy Days, Egypt invaded Israel across the Suez Canal, and Syria attacked the Golan Heights. Israel ultimately defended itself but suffered heavy losses. Meir took responsibility for the country's relatively unprepared state. Soon after, she stepped down. "I am exhausted," she said simply. "I can no longer carry the burden. I have reached the end of the road."

Golda Meir is remembered for her total devotion to her people and her dedication to their survival. "The Jewish people can be led to the gas chambers," she said. "They destroyed their minds and their bodies, but never their spirit..... We always have faith, always believe."

took on issues of poverty, health care, and peace, and edited the church magazine, *Social Progress*. Throughout the 1940s, '50s, and '60s, she was an activist for desegregation, affordable housing, peace, and national health care.

At the time the Gray Panthers were founded, few people publicly questioned the routine marginalization of old people. Kuhn and the Panthers popularized the idea that ageism is a social poison as repugnant as sexism or racism. The group was originally called the Consultation of Older and Younger Adults for Social Change, until a journalist compared them with the Black Panthers. Kuhn welcomed the comparison, and embraced the new name. "Gray is a symbolic color," she said. "Everyone gets old, and if you put all the colors of the rainbow together you get gray." The group's goal was nothing less than "fundamental social change that would eliminate injustice, discrimination

Left: Gray Panthers founder Maggie Kuhn in 1981. **Below:** Kuhn organizing in Philadelphia. **Opposite:** Vietnamese negotiator Nguyen Thi Binh at the Paris peace talks in 1971.

Maggie Kuhn
activist (1905–1995)

When Maggie Kuhn was forced to retire at age sixty-five from a job she had excelled at for twenty-five years, she didn't agonize—she organized. She got together with four women friends and, in 1970, they started the Gray Panthers, a radical group that agitates to end age discrimination and other forms of injustice.

Before Kuhn was born, her parents had moved to Buffalo from Memphis because they did not want to raise their child in the segregated South. The family eventually moved to Cleveland, and Kuhn earned her college degree from Case Western Reserve University, where she organized a chapter of the League of Women Voters.

In the late 1930s, Kuhn worked for the social education and action department of the United Presbyterian Church, where she and oppression in our present society"; its slogan was "Age and Youth in Action."

The Panthers started out campaigning against the Vietnam War, setting the tone for their future intergenerational emphasis. They also successfully lobbied for legislation on nursing home reform, protested demeaning portrayals of old people in the media, called for universal access to health care, defended Social Security, helped pass the Age Discrimination in Employment Act, and generally raised consciousness about ageism. "The first myth is that old age is a disease, a terrible disease that you never admit you've got, so you lie about your age," said Kuhn. "Well, it's not a disease, it's a triumph, because you've survived. Failure, disappointment, sickness, loss—you're still here."

Kuhn traveled all around the United States, tirelessly organizing, speaking, and lobbying. She promoted intergenerational housing arrangements and shared her own home with a group of people of different ages. She wrote three books—*Get Out There and Do Something About Injustice*; *Maggie Kuhn on Ageing*; and her autobiography, *No Stone Unturned*.

Kuhn never married, and she was open about her many affairs, including a fifteen-year relationship with a married minister and a liaison with a man fifty years her junior. She was unapologetic about her identity and her mission. "I am an old woman," she said. "I have gray hair, many wrinkles, and arthritis in both hands. And I celebrate my freedom from bureaucratic restraints that once held me."

Nguyen Thi Binh
political activist (1927–)

For Nguyen Thi Binh, a chief negotiator of the Paris peace accord that ended the Vietnam war, one point was not negotiable. "A cease-fire is not enough," she said. "It must go together with withdrawal of all United States troops from South Vietnam." Fiercely nationalistic, Binh represented the National Liberation Front (NLF), the influential cadre of more than one million Vietnamese peasant resistance fighters. Having ascended to the vice presidency of Vietnam, she has been a major political figure in her country for almost fifty years.

Born into a middle-class, politically active family in Saigon, Binh hated the French occupation of her country. "I profoundly resented the fact that we were taught Vietnamese as a secondary language to French," she said. In 1946, she joined the anti-France student movement and five years later was arrested and jailed for taking part in a public protest against the French. Binh was tortured with electric shock periodically during her three-year imprisonment. She was released following the signing of the 1954 Geneva peace accord, which divided Vietnam into the North and South regions.

When South Vietnam's President Ngo Dinh Diem refused to hold national elections as called for by the Geneva accord, guerrilla fighting broke out throughout the countryside. Binh and her husband, Luu Van Nhon, joined the opposition movement that organized scattered bands of resistance fighters into a massive, well-coordinated army known as the National Liberation Front

(also known pejoratively as the Viet Cong). An ardent feminist, Binh chaired the NLF's Women's Liberation Association and recruited peasant women to its ranks with the promise of equal rights; the women became spies, political activists, combat soldiers, and medical personnel.

Known as "the flower and fire of the revolution," Binh was appointed minister of foreign affairs for the Provisional Revolutionary Government (PRG) of South Vietnam in 1969. When North Vietnam tentatively agreed to commence peace talks with the United States, Binh was given a place at the table. She dismissed President Diem as heading a U.S.-backed puppet government, contending that she was "the true representative of South Vietnamese aspirations" and in a position to negotiate a cease-fire. Playing hardball, she insisted on complete withdrawal of U.S. troops and called for the formation of a coalition government and the eventual reunification of Vietnam. Binh had to concede on several points, but she held her ground on the U.S. troop withdrawal. After signing the accord on January 27, 1973, she said, "If you asked us who is the winner, we would like to say, peace is the winner."

When North Vietnam and South Vietnam reunified as the Socialist Republic of Vietnam in 1976, Binh was named minister of education, a post she held for more than ten years. In 1992, she was elected vice president of Vietnam. "People ask why I am in politics," she mused late in her career. "If you mean by politics, the fight for the right to live, then we do it because we are obligated to. But fighting for that is not politics. It is much more fundamental."

Billie Jean King
athlete (1943–)

On September 20, 1973, a live audience of more than thirty thousand people, along with sixty million television viewers, watched in anxious anticipation as Billie Jean King, the reigning Wimbledon champion, and Bobby Riggs, a fifty-five-year-old former tennis pro, stepped onto the court. The winner of this match would receive $100,000 in prize money, but everyone knew there was much more at stake in this competition.

Riggs had challenged King as a challenge to "women's lib," bragging that women were so inferior to men that no woman could beat a man. King, meanwhile, was leading a campaign by women tennis players to win equal respect—and pay—to that of men. Her massively publicized trouncing of Riggs was a memorable lesson to women and men around the world about the power and potential of women, and it strengthened her quest to achieve parity for women players.

King had been an athletic prodigy growing up in a family of modest means in Long Beach, California. "When I was five or six," she said, "I told my mother I'd be the best in something; by the time I was twelve, I knew what I'd be the best in." King first stepped onto the grass court at Wimbledon at the age of seventeen, as half of the youngest team ever to win the women's doubles title; five years later, she won her first singles tournament there. In 1967 and 1973, she won Wimbledon's triple crown,

Above: Billie Jean King competing in 1974 at Wimbledon, where she won a record twenty titles. **Opposite:** Billie Jean King in 1981.

capturing the women's singles, women's doubles, and mixed doubles titles.

Drawing on her extraordinary strength, unusual speed, and lightning-fast reflexes, Billie Jean King won dozens of tournaments around the world: in singles, doubles, and mixed doubles; on clay, grass, carpet, and hard court—including a record twenty Wimbledon titles.

King was a fierce competitor and became just as fiercely committed to fairness for female athletes. In the 1960s and early 1970s, all the tennis associations treated women as secondary acts. King brought an unprecedented feminist consciousness to sports, bravely putting her reputation and her career on the line by speaking out, organizing other players to boycott tournaments where the pay inequities were most egregious, and traveling around the country promoting the worth of women as professional athletes.

Her message was simple but revolutionary. Women athletes, she said, wanted "recognition as athletes, pros, not for our looks. Do the reporters care if a football player is ugly as long as he can block, tackle, and do his job? An athlete has to perform. Measure us that way; not on sex."

In 1971, there was $250,000 in prize money to be won by women tennis players. That same year, King became the first woman in the sport to earn more than $100,000 in a year. By the time she retired, in 1984, women tennis pros were collectively taking home $11 million.

In 1973, King became the founder and first president of the Women's Tennis Association. She was also a founder of the Women's Sports Foundation and *womenSports* magazine, which later became *Women's Sports and Fitness.* As founder and director of World TeamTennis, which organizes recreational and professional leagues, King continues to be an ambassador for the game and an advocate for the value of sports in girls' and women's lives. Largely because of her personal efforts and unwavering commitment, the sport she loves now enjoys world-class status and popularity.

Barbara Walters

journalist (1931–)

From her start as the *Today Show* "girl" to her achievement as the highest-paid journalist in television, world-renowned interviewer Barbara Walters got there the old-fashioned way. "I didn't have blazing talent, or marvelous beauty," she said. "I got to where I am by hard work and perseverance." Perched on the edge of her chair, index cards stacked neatly in her hands, Walters leans forward and coaxes surprisingly intimate revelations out of even the most stalwart subjects. Often scooping her colleagues, Walters continues to make news with ground-breaking, timely interviews that air on the top-rated Barbara Walters specials and the popular weekly newsmagazine *20/20*.

Walters has interviewed every U.S. president since Richard Nixon and landed exclusives with world figures such as Robert Kennedy, Golda Meir, Coretta Scott King, and the Shah of Iran. Her coups include an hour-long conversation with Cuba's President Fidel Castro (after which he inscribed a photo to her, "As a remembrance of the most difficult interview that I have had in all the days of my life"), the first joint interview of Egypt's President Anwar Sadat and Israel's Prime Minister Menachim Begin, and an award-winning interview with well-loved actor Christopher Reeve after a riding accident had left him paralyzed. Walters has been criticized for being too soft on her subjects, but her disarmingly simple and direct questions frequently elicit very personal answers. "I don't do silly, giddy interviews," she bristles. She makes a clear distinction between hard-news journalism (she won't interview a movie star on *20/20*) and celebrity schmooze-fests. Perhaps what unnerves her critics is her palpable empathy with her subjects.

The daughter of Boston nightclub impresario Lou Walters, she grew up in the show-biz worlds of Boston, Miami, and New York City. After graduating from Sarah Lawrence College in 1953, she held a series of entry-level jobs in television news. In 1961, Walters was hired as a writer for the popular NBC *Today Show*, and after three years, she was given a chance on-air in the traditionally decorative role of "*Today* Girl." Seizing the opportunity, she impressed network executives with solid reporting, clear intelligence, and a strong camera presence. She eventually became a regular commentator and news reader and, in 1974, joined Hugh Downs as co-host of the *Today Show*.

Two years later, Walters made history by landing a five-year contract with rival network ABC, becoming the first woman to co-anchor a network evening news program, and, with a yearly salary of $1 million, the highest-paid journalist ever. The pairing was a public and painful failure—her co-anchor, Harry Reasoner, barely disguised his resentment, and the program did not attract the audience ABC had hoped for. To salvage her contract, ABC assigned her to do her own one-hour programs, and *The Barbara Walters Special* was born.

"There are not too many people who've been working at this as long as I have and at the level I have—and are still going," she noted recently. The tenacious Walters is easing up a bit, but don't count her out. "I don't want to tell you that if there was a hot news interview, I wouldn't go in a second," she said. "The difference is if I don't get it, I don't sit up at night."

Below: Barbara Walters with Lauren Bacall at a tribute to colleague Sam Donaldson. **Opposite:** Barbara Walters broke through as a serious reporter at a time when women were usually valued only as set decoration.

Margaret Thatcher

prime minister (1925–)

Great Britain's first female prime minister, Margaret Thatcher, known as the "Iron Lady," transformed her country's social and economic policies with characteristic singleness of purpose. "To me," said Thatcher, "consensus seems to be the process of abandoning all beliefs, principles, values, and policies in search of something in which no one believes, but to which no one objects." Elected in 1979 and ruling for more than a decade, she overhauled England's social welfare system, shifted state-owned industries to the private sector, and broke the once-powerful labor unions. Holding the office of prime minister longer than anyone in the nation's history, Thatcher became one of the most powerful world leaders of her time.

The daughter of a grocer and a dressmaker, she studied chemistry at Oxford University and then attended law school. After practicing tax law for a number of years, she was elected to Parliament in 1959. When Prime Minister Edward Heath made her education secretary in 1970, she became the first and only woman cabinet member in his administration. Forced to cut the budget, she eliminated free milk in the schools for children older than eight years of age, earning the nickname "Mrs. Thatcher, milk snatcher." She stood her ground, displaying the defiance that would typify her leadership.

Succeeding Heath as the leader of the Conservative party in 1974, Thatcher became prime minister when the Conservatives carried the election four years later. She has said that at the time she took office, England "was a country in decline. Poor in spirit, we suffered from that most demoralizing form of poverty—poverty of conviction. Britain was a country without a cause." Thatcher seized the moment, setting an agenda of spending cuts, union-bashing, capitalism, patriotism, and individual responsibility that came to be known as "Thatcherism."

Fiercely antisocialist, she severely cut services to the poor while promoting tight spending, private-sector solutions to public problems, and a free-enterprise economy with strictly controlled inflation. Her first year in office, unemployment doubled and her party's public approval dropped precipitously. Thatcher's popularity bounced back up with the 1982 British victory in the Falkland Islands war. By her second term, she had

144

Below: Margaret Thatcher enjoys a spin in a tank in a training area in Fallingbostel, West Germany, where she visited British and West German troops in 1986. **Opposite:** Thatcher in 1987.

slashed inflation from twenty-two percent to four percent, income taxes were reduced (particularly for the upper-income bracket), and she had boosted the economy through the sale to private industry of more than $50 billion worth of government assets, including British Gas, British Telecom, and British Airways.

After ten years at the helm, Thatcher had difficulty articulating a clear vision for the future. As the rapidly changing European community demanded flexibility and new paradigms for coexisting, she became more entrenched. "The lady's not for turning," she said. "I will not change just to court popularity." In November of 1990, the woman who had reinvented England resigned as prime minister.

Roseanne
actor and producer (1952–)

As a housewife living in a Colorado trailer park with her husband and three kids, Roseanne dared to believe that her reality was important and entertaining. She anointed herself a "domestic goddess" and brought down the house at local comedy clubs with her droll delivery of everyday triumphs: "I figure when my husband comes home from work, if the kids are still alive, then I've done my job." As the creator and star of the phenomenally successful sitcom *Roseanne*, based on her life, she forever changed the expectations of television audiences by presenting real, complex, working-class characters and their struggles. "I just wanted to hold a mirror up to the society we live in," she said, "and I really wanted to honor what was ordinary and yet extraordinary about moms and family."

A Molotov cocktail of guts and talent mixed with rage, Roseanne wrested control over her show from a string of network executives and producers to hold fast to her vision, making her one of the most powerful and wealthiest women in Hollywood. "No one has really been able to replicate the family or class thing on television, and you know why?" she said. "Because none of 'em are from there."

Born Roseanne Barr, she was raised in a Jewish family in the Mormon hub of Salt Lake City, Utah. She dropped out of high school, got pregnant, gave up her daughter for adoption (they

were later reunited), and then headed for the mountains of Colorado, where she lived for several years in an artists' colony.

Roseanne got married young, to motel night clerk Bill Pentland, and had three more children. She worked part-time as a wisecracking cocktail waitress; her customers urged her to take her show on the road. She conquered local comedy clubs and the L.A. club scene in rapid succession. Roseanne hit the big time in August of 1985, with a guest spot on *The Tonight Show* with Johnny Carson. Three years later, she had her own show.

For nine years, audiences tuned in to watch the fumblings and foibles of the contentious Conners, who hip-checked the seamless Cosbys out of the number-one slot in the first season. Surrounded by an exquisite ensemble cast featuring John

Goodman, Laurie Metcalf, and Sara Gilbert, Roseanne demonstrated that fat can be sexy, that not having money shapes everything, that being a parent can suck, and that the more you tease a person, the more you love 'em. Fearless and feminist, she brought to life the slogan "The personal is political," taking on the issues of abortion, sexuality, poverty, racism, and sexism.

After divorcing Pentland, Roseanne married her second husband, actor Tom Arnold, in 1990, and together they careened around town like an out-of-control roller coaster ride. Their split in 1994 was no prettier. "I'm not upset about my divorce," Roseanne said, "I'm only upset that I'm not a widow." Her third marriage, to bodyguard Ben Thomas, with whom she had a son, Buck, ended in 1998.

"I'm pretty done with television for a while," she said as her show came to an end, "though I might come back to it. But I'd like to shake up another medium, and maybe one after that, and maybe one after that. I'd like to be pushy, and blow up as much as I can."

Hanan Ashrawi
political leader (1946–)

Hanan Ashrawi has spent her adult life fighting for Palestinian self-determination and working within Palestinian society for women's equality, human rights, and democracy. As a Palestine Liberation Organization (PLO) official and as an independent political leader, she has been committed to resolving the stubborn problem of a just peace in the Middle East. "In the moment that I give up hope," she said, "I will not be in the peace process. If we lose faith, there will be no peaceful solution to the conflict. Peace will be very difficult and very painful, but I think we have to do it."

The daughter of a prominent physician, she grew up under Jordanian rule in Ramallah, on the West Bank. She was studying at the American University of Beirut in 1967 when Israel occupied the Gaza Strip and the West Bank. "After the 1967 war, the 'Palestinian Question'—whether we would ever have our land restored to us, or at least a portion of it—had become a personal issue," Ashrawi wrote in her memoir, *This Side of Peace*. "With the occupation of the West Bank and Gaza, it had hit home, literally."

Barred by the Israeli military government from returning to her home, she went to the University of Virginia to study for a doctorate in medieval literature. In 1973, she was finally allowed to go back to Ramallah, where she became head of the English department at Birzeit University and joined students in demonstrating against the occupation. In 1975, she married Emile Ashrawi, a photographer and former rock drummer; they have two daughters.

In the PLO, Ashrawi has always been admittedly an "outsider"—female, wealthy, Christian, feminist, and United States–educated. But her intelligence and savvy were recognized

Above: Hanan Ashrawi in 1992.

by PLO Chairman Yasser Arafat, and eventually she became a close aide and adviser to him. In 1988, during the *Intifada*—the Palestinian uprising in the West Bank and Gaza Strip—Ashrawi emerged as an impressive spokesperson.

During the 1991 Middle East peace conference in Madrid, she represented the Palestinian viewpoint to the world. Ultimately, Arafat and Israeli Prime Minister Yitzhak Rabin signed a peace accord as a result of separate, secret negotiations conducted in Oslo. The Oslo agreement granted Palestinians limited self-rule in the Gaza Strip and certain areas of the West Bank. Ashrawi, deeply disappointed in its limited scope, refused to sign the accord and turned down Arafat's invitation to join the newly formed Palestinian Authority, saying, "We don't want simply to reorganize the occupation, with the Palestinians taking over some of the functions of the occupiers."

In 1993, concerned with human rights violations in the occupied territories, Ashrawi resigned from the PLO and started the Palestinian Independent Commission for Citizens' Rights, whose mandate she characterized as "laying down the foundations of a genuine democracy, safeguarding people's rights, and ensuring the rule of law." Three years later she won a seat on the Palestinian Legislative Council and then became education minister for the Palestinian National Authority.

Oprah Winfrey
talk show host, actor, and producer (1954–)

*T*he world's highest-paid entertainer, Oprah Winfrey never doubted that she would reach the top. "All my life I have always known I was born to greatness," she said. Judging from her inauspicious beginnings, she may have been the only one who knew.

Born in Kosciusko, Mississippi, to unmarried teenage parents, Winfrey had an unsettled and unhappy childhood. She first lived in poverty on her grandmother's farm. From the age of six she stayed off and on with her mother in Milwaukee, where she was sexually abused as a child by male relatives. At fourteen, she gave birth to a premature baby who didn't survive. She then went to live with her father and stepmother in

Below: Oprah Winfrey is moved to tears as she testifies on child abuse before the Senate Judiciary Committee in 1991.

Nashville. In the more structured, disciplined atmosphere of their home, Oprah at last began to thrive, excelling at school and even skipping several grades.

She earned a scholarship to Tennessee State University and, while still in school, became co-anchor of the evening news at WTF-TV. In 1984, after eight years at Baltimore's WJZ-TV, where she hosted a talk show, *People Are Talking*, Winfrey moved to Chicago to host the ABC affiliate's morning talk show, *AM Chicago*. She took the job with some trepidation, since the program ran opposite talk-show titan Phil Donahue. Instead of trying to out-Donahue Donahue, Winfrey decided to just be herself. Her warm, personal style charmed guests and audiences alike, and, astonishingly, within three months, she was beating

Donahue in the ratings. By 1985, her program, renamed *The Oprah Winfrey Show*, was expanded to an hour, and the following year it was launched in national syndication.

Winfrey has shared her own secrets and heartaches and, murmuring like a confidante, asked the most intimate questions of both guests and audience members. "I don't try to change people," she said. "I try to expose them for what they are." With almost twenty million viewers and twenty-five Emmy awards, *The Oprah Winfrey Show* is hugely successful for its star and for its distributor, King World Productions.

In 1985, Winfrey also made her impressive acting debut, as the feisty Sofia in the film adaptation of Alice Walker's *The Color Purple*, and was nominated for an Oscar for best supporting actress. Soon thereafter, she formed her own production company, Harpo Productions, and began producing *The Oprah Winfrey Show*. She negotiated a lucrative syndication deal and set about acquiring the film and television rights to the works of important African-American writers.

In the meantime, the successful format of Winfrey's and Donahue's shows spawned cheap, sensational imitations that inevitably went for the lowest common denominator, in choice of topics and guest alike, and eventually the airwaves were flooded by what came to be known as "trash TV." In 1994, Winfrey revamped her show to focus on positive, compelling subjects. One of her most popular features is her book club, in which she selects a book and gives her audience time to read it before the author appears as a guest on the show. Promoting literacy and education, this book club has also helped to lift a flagging publishing industry; every book she has recommended has become an instant bestseller.

Now worth half a billion dollars, Winfrey is a lavish philanthropist, primarily funding educational institutions and programs to help kids. Through perseverance, talent, and her unmatched ability to connect with people, Winfrey has become one of the best-loved television personalities and a true media powerhouse.

Below: Oprah Winfrey makes a grand entrance at the 67th Annual Academy Awards, 1995.

149

LASTING LEGACY

Mary McLeod Bethune, educator

Margaret Sanger, birth control pioneer

Martha Graham, dancer and choreographer

Mildred "Babe" Didrikson Zaharias, athlete

Eleanor Roosevelt, humanitarian

Anne Frank, diarist

Rosie the Riveter, working woman

Lucille Ball, actor and producer

Marilyn Monroe, actor

Clara McBride Hale, child care pioneer

Gloria Steinem, activist and writer

Gladys Tantaquidgeon, anthropologist and medicine woman

Diana, Princess of Wales, humanitarian

———⚬⚬⚬⚬———

Larger than life, these memorable women have an instinctive gift for touching people's lives in ways that transcend their times and circumstances. Their profound impact will continue to be felt well into the twenty-first century.

Lucille Ball

Gloria Steinem

Eleanor Roosevelt

"Babe" Didrikson Zaharias

Anne Frank

Martha Graham

Margaret Sanger

Maril...

Mary McLeod Bethune

Mary McLeod Bethune

educator (1875–1955)

a devout Christian with a mission, Mary McLeod Bethune believed in God and believed in herself. "Without faith, nothing is possible," she said. "With it, nothing is impossible." In 1895, her dream to travel to Africa as a missionary was dashed—the Presbyterian Mission Board denied her application because it did not allow African Americans to serve in Africa. Bethune instead used her considerable talents as an educator and natural abilities as a leader to improve the lives and status of black people in the United States. For more than three decades, Bethune, a dazzling orator and skillful negotiator, was the most visible and influential black woman in the nation.

Born into a family of seventeen children in Mayesville, South Carolina, the daughter of former slaves didn't learn to read until age eleven, when a mission school with a black instructor opened near her home. With a scholarship, in 1888 she enrolled in Scotia Seminary, where a faculty of black and white teachers laid the foundation for her lifelong optimism about improving race relations. After graduating from Chicago's Moody Bible Institute, she taught in several small southern schools. In 1904, she moved to Daytona, Florida, with her new husband, Albertus Bethune, and their infant son, to open a school near a large railway construction project. As legend has it, with only one dollar and fifty cents and an infinite amount of faith, she opened the Daytona Normal and Industrial Institute for Negro Girls with the motto "Enter to learn, depart to serve."

Although the school began with no assets or supplies—the six original students had box cartons for desks and crushed elderberries for ink—Bethune rustled up financial support from much of the black community and convinced white philanthropists to donate to her institute. In less than twenty years, the Daytona Normal and Industrial School had grown into a lovely twenty-acre campus with eight buildings and a farm, a student body of three hundred girls, a staff of twenty-five, and a flourishing teacher-training program. The school also sponsored the establishment of a much-needed community hospital.

The next step was to expand the school into a college. In 1923, it merged with Cookman Institute for Men and, in 1929, was rechristened Bethune-Cookman College. Bethune led the college as president from 1923 to 1942, earning its full accreditation and increasing its enrollment to more than one thousand

... tional prominence. A close
... he became a national advi-
... klin D. Roosevelt.
... f women and girls—
... red by the character of
... re she had founded the
... tion of powerful black
... ntil 1949 and was vice
... her death in 1955.

Below: Mary McLeod Bethune (seated), accompanied by a delegation from Bethune-Cookman College, visits President Roosevelt's mother.

Margaret Sanger
birth control pioneer (1879–1966)

*I*n 1910, when Margaret Sanger started working as a visiting nurse in the slums of Manhattan's Lower East Side, it was illegal to sell contraceptive devices. In fact, the term "birth control" didn't exist until Sanger coined it, convinced that the ability to choose whether to have children was the key to women's control of their lives. She devoted her life to making reproductive freedom a reality for American women.

Margaret's parents influenced her destiny in very different ways. Her father, a radical thinker, encouraged her intellect with lively discussions. But she was troubled by her mother's life, believing it had been cut short by the strain of bearing and raising eleven children with little help from Margaret's father. Having trained as an obstetrical nurse in the New York City suburbs, she married architect William Sanger in 1902, and they later moved to Manhattan with their three children.

Ministering to poor women, Sanger dealt with the tragic consequences of unwanted children and self-induced abortions. She was outraged at the lack of reproductive choices available to poor women and at the suppression of badly needed information about sexuality, sexual health, sexually transmitted diseases, and contraception. "No woman can call herself free who does not own and control her body," she later wrote. "No woman can call herself free until she can choose consciously whether she will or will not be a mother."

In 1914, Sanger started a militant feminist journal, *The Woman Rebel*, which promoted free love, the workers' revolution, and women's liberation. Even though *The Woman Rebel* contained no contraceptive information, Sanger was quickly indicted under repressive obscenity laws. On the eve of her trial, she left for Europe, where she studied approaches to family planning in var-

Above: Margaret Sanger (center, holding portfolio) organizing with other prominent birth control advocates in 1929.

ious countries. Soon after she returned to the United States in 1915, the obscenity case against her was dropped.

In 1916, she and her sister, Ethel Byrne, opened the first birth control center in the United States. Their Brooklyn clinic was shut down by the police within ten days. The two women were jailed, but their case led to a ruling that allowed doctors to give advice about contraceptives to their patients. This ruling fell far short of making birth control widely accessible, but Sanger used the doctors' provision as a wedge, establishing birth control clinics staffed by doctors. In 1923, she started the Birth Control Clinical Research Bureau, a clinic that not only trained doctors and provided contraceptive information to women, but also conducted the first systematic clinical tests of the effectiveness of various birth control methods. By 1938, Sanger and her colleagues had established more than three hundred such clinics.

She divorced William Sanger in 1920 and, two years later, married millionaire J. Noah Slee, who bankrolled her activities. In 1921, Sanger founded the American Birth Control League, which later became the Planned Parenthood Federation of America, one of the most respected family planning organizations in the world. In 1937, the American Medical Association finally called for training in contraception in medical schools, a big step toward Sanger's goal "to raise the question of birth control out of the gutter of obscenity...into the light of intelligence and human understanding."

Below: Adhering dramatically to a ruling that she must not preach about birth control in Boston, Margaret Sanger wears adhesive tape over her mouth to attend a 1929 dinner there. She wrote her views on a blackboard at the event.
Opposite: Martha Graham.

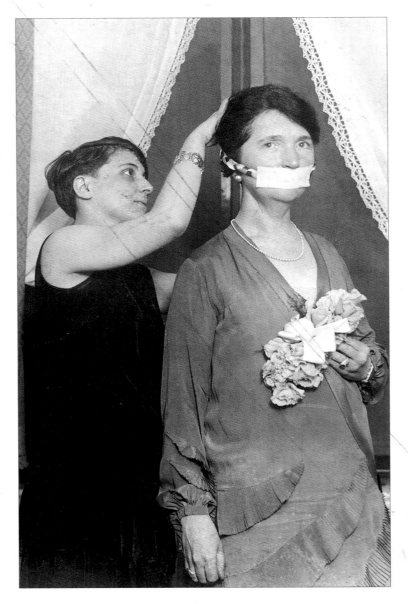

Martha Graham
dancer and choreographer (1894–1991)

One of the founders of modern dance, Martha Graham answered a higher calling. "I did not choose to be a dancer," she wrote. "I was chosen." Her revolutionary ideas about dance broke away from the movements and techniques of classical ballet and created a completely new art form. Withstanding the stinging criticism that often greets innovation, Graham courageously pursued her vision. She choreographed more than 180 dramatic works in her lifetime, leaving a profound and indelible imprint on twentieth-century dance.

After her early training with influential dance pioneers Ruth St. Denis and Ted Shawn in Los Angeles and then New York, Graham taught at the Eastman School of Theatre in Rochester, New York, from 1924 to 1925. There she began to develop her own style. In April 1926, she premiered to critical acclaim in New York City as a solo dancer in pieces that she created. The next year, she founded the Martha Graham School of Contemporary Dance in New York and began a lifelong exploration of the expressive power of dance techniques based on the contraction and release of the torso. Used to the graceful, flowing movements of ballet, early audiences and critics laughed nervously at her dance troupe, finding their movements jarring and ugly. Graham was unfazed. "It's not my job to look beautiful," she told her students. "It's my job to look interesting."

Graham's early works, such as *Primitive Mysteries*, *Incantation*, and *Dolorosa*, incorporated her intrigue with the culture of Mexican Indians. In 1932, she studied in Mexico as the first dancer ever awarded a Guggenheim fellowship.

Often accompanied by original musical compositions, Graham created a body of work that featured uniquely American themes, as in *Appalachian Spring* (to the music of Aaron Copland), *Frontier*, and *Letter to the World*, inspired by the life and poetry of Emily Dickinson. Striving to express inner tensions and reveal the conflicts of the soul, Graham often chose powerful women from history and Greek mythology, such as Medea, Phaedra, Persephone, Joan of Arc, and the Brontë sisters, as archetypes in her works.

Through her indefatigable efforts and astonishing talent, Graham was able to establish modern dance as a legitimate art form. "No artist is ahead of his time," she said. "He *is* his time; it is just that others are behind the time." Dancing well into her seventies, she retired from performing in 1969, although she continued to choreograph and direct her school until her death at age ninety-six.

Her compelling style—dancers draped in flowing garments executing angular movements and arching kicks—is instantly identifiable. "There is a vitality, a life-force, an energy, a quickening that is translated through you into action," Graham explained, "and because there is only one of you in all of time, this expression is unique."

Below: Choreographer Martha Graham demonstrates her original technique at a 1927 dance class in Boston. **Right:** Babe Didrikson Zaharias.

Mildred "Babe" Didrikson Zaharias
athlete (1911–1956)

Even as a kid playing sandlot baseball with the boys, Mildred Didrikson was an amazing athlete. Her playmates in her working-class neighborhood in Beaumont, Texas, called her Babe after baseball legend Babe Ruth. As a high school basketball star, she once scored 104 points in a game. She went on to enjoy an athletic career unparalleled in its accomplishments and versatility, excelling in track and field, basketball, baseball, bowling, golf, tennis, and diving. "All I know," she once said, "is that I can run and I can jump and I can toss things."

Before she had finished high school, Didrikson was recruited to work at Employers Casualty Company in Dallas as a typist so that she could play for the company-sponsored women's basketball team, which played under the auspices of the Amateur Athletic Union (AAU). In her first game for the Golden Cyclones, she dazzled her new teammates by scoring more points alone than the other team did all together. A three-time All-American, Didrikson led the team to two finals and one national championship.

Didrikson also competed in AAU track and field meets for Employers Casualty, mastering shot put, discus, javelin, high jump, long jump, hurdles, and baseball throw. At the 1932 AAU championships, she competed in eight events, winning five, tying one, and racking up more points than the entire twenty-two-member second-place team. Later that year, she took home three medals from the Los Angeles Olympics—gold in javelin and hurdles, silver in high jump.

In 1932, she decided to take up golf, a game she would come to dominate as both an amateur and a professional. Brash, proud, and flamboyant, Didrikson brought a new level of showmanship to the rarefied, country club atmosphere of women's golf. After she won the 1935 Texas Women's Amateur Championship, the United States Golf Association declared her a professional. Since there were only two pro tournaments for women at the time, she spent several years playing in exhibition games, often with some of the leading male golfers in the world. In 1944, her amateur status was reinstated, and two years later she won the U.S. Women's Amateur Tournament. She went on to win seventeen tournaments in a row.

In 1938, she married professional wrestler George Zaharias, who became her manager. In order to create more professional opportunities for women golfers, she helped found the Ladies Professional Golf Association (LPGA) in 1949. Zaharias went on to win thirty-one of its tournaments, becoming the LPGA's top money winner in 1949, 1950, and 1951. In the midst of a string of victories, Zaharias was diagnosed with colon cancer. She returned to competition three and a half months after undergoing a colostomy and won the U.S. Open in 1954. But the cancer recurred in 1955, and she died the following year. One of the greatest athletes of all time, Zaharias not only achieved extraordinary personal triumphs, she also brought a new level of professionalism and respect to women's sports.

Below: After winning three gold medals in the 1932 Olympics, Zaharias returned to her secretarial job at a Dallas insurance company.

Eleanor Roosevelt
humanitarian (1884–1962)

a tally of Eleanor Roosevelt's achievements seems overwhelming, even unreal: First Lady; United Nations delegate; champion of human rights; mother of six; peacemaker; civil rights lobbyist; writer; and advocate for the poor, the ill, and the oppressed. The scope of her influence in the United States and the world is immeasurable.

Anna Eleanor Roosevelt had a lonely childhood. An orphan by age ten, she was raised in New York City by her emotionally cold grandmother until being sent off to boarding school in England. Yet Roosevelt's lifetime commitment to helping other people started early on; at eighteen, she was already volunteering at a settlement house. "Usefulness," she said, "whatever form it may take, is the price we should pay for the air we breathe and the food we eat and the privilege of being alive."

In 1905, she married her distant cousin Franklin Delano Roosevelt, an ambitious law student. For years, she focused on rearing their six children and on furthering his political career. Her hopes of forging a true romantic partnership with her husband were shattered in 1918, when she found out he was having an affair with her social secretary. Over time, their marriage evolved into more of a respectful working relationship. After FDR was paralyzed by polio in 1921, she traveled throughout New York state performing many of his official duties as governor.

When her husband became president of the United States in 1932, Eleanor Roosevelt immediately redefined the role of First Lady. She regularly held press conferences for female journalists. She helped bring women into the administration. And because of FDR's disability, she took on a uniquely active public role. It is said that she served as his eyes, ears, and legs as she traveled throughout the country, visiting poverty-stricken neighborhoods, inspecting government works projects,

talking with coal miners and garment workers and Appalachian farmers and unemployed people. She would bring their stories back to the White House and advocate with the president for relief. Her lobbying wasn't always successful, but she was a strong voice for people who previously had none.

Roosevelt kept the country informed about her activities and her political views through a syndicated newspaper column called "My Day" and numerous radio broadcasts. The First Lady was also the major advocate within the White House for African-American civil rights. She urged her husband to end racial discrimination in the military and to support a law that would have made lynching a federal crime. In 1939, she resigned from

Above: Eleanor Roosevelt happily acknowledges the cheering crowd as she addresses the 1960 Democratic National Convention. **Opposite:** U.S. First Lady Eleanor Roosevelt.

the Daughters of the American Revolution because of its refusal to allow black opera singer Marian Anderson to perform. That same year she became a member of the National Association for the Advancement of Colored People.

After FDR's death in 1945, she kept up her advocacy, lobbying President Harry S Truman on civil rights, labor laws, and fair U.S. foreign policy. Truman appointed her as a delegate to the United Nations and, in 1946, she became the chair of the U.N. Commission on Human Rights. She resigned that post in 1953 but for the remainder of her life continued to travel around the world, advocating for human rights.

In addition to her mind-boggling array of accomplishments, Eleanor Roosevelt created a new model for the possibilities of women in public life, working in both official and unofficial capacities to open the door to expanded human rights for everyone. "I have spent many years of my life in opposition, and I rather like the role," she wrote in 1952. Through the Depression, the New Deal, and World War II, she was the most prominent,

admired, and influential American woman, and her legacy of justice, perseverance, and tireless advocacy reverberates today.

Anne Frank
diarist (1929–1945)

*In spite of everything, I still believe that people are
really good at heart.*

Wise far beyond her tender years, Anne Frank wrote poignantly of her coming of age in her diary. "It's an odd idea for someone like me to keep a diary," she wrote, "not only because I have never done so before, but because it seems to me that neither I—nor for that matter anyone else—will be interested in the unbosomings of a thirteen-year-old schoolgirl." In fact, her chatty adolescent musings were remarkable in their insight into the human condition—made all the more extraordinary because she wrote them throughout the two years she and her family hid from the Nazis in an Amsterdam attic. Published a few years after her death at the Bergen-Belsen concentration camp in 1945, Anne Frank's diary is an important historical chronicle of the Holocaust and a mere glimpse of the brilliant mind and indomitable spirit that was so brutally extinguished.

Sometimes I believe that God wants to try me, both now and later on; I must become good through my own efforts, without examples and without good advice. Then later on I shall be all the stronger. Who besides me will ever read these letters? From whom but myself shall I get comfort? As I need comforting often, I frequently feel weak, and dissatisfied with myself; my shortcomings are too great. I know this, and every day I try to improve myself, again and again.

Anne's Jewish parents fled their homeland of Germany in 1933 with their two daughters, Anne and her older sister, Margot, to escape the Nazis. Her father, Otto, reestablished his pharmaceuticals business in Amsterdam, but the Germans occupied the Netherlands in 1941. Rather than leave their adopted country, the Franks went into hiding to avoid capture. For two years, they subsisted in a tiny attic above Otto Frank's offices, along with the Van Daans and their teenage son, Peter, and a dentist named Albert Dussel.

My treatment varies so much. One day Anne is so sensible and is allowed to know everything; and the next day I hear that Anne is just a silly little goat who doesn't know anything at all and imagines that she's learned a wonderful lot from books. I'm not a baby or a spoiled darling any more, to be laughed at, whatever she does. I have my own views, plans, and ideas, though I can't put them into words yet. Oh, so many things bubble up inside me as I lie in bed, having to put up with people I'm fed up with, who always misinterpret my intentions.

Writing in the form of letters addressed "Dear Kitty," Anne poured her heart and her troubles into her diary: her friction with her mother, her struggle for the affection of her father, her burgeoning interest in Peter, and her annoyance with the extended cast of characters who shared the "Secret Annexe" with her.

She wrote movingly of the unremitting terror of being discovered and the snippets of war news that increased their foreboding.

That's why in the end I always come back to my diary. That is where I start and finish, because Kitty is always patient. I'll promise her that I shall persevere, in spite of everything, and find my own way through it all, and swallow my tears. I only wish I could see the results already or occasionally receive encouragement from someone who loves me.

Their hiding place was eventually discovered by the Gestapo, and everyone was deported to Bergen-Belsen; Otto Frank was the lone survivor of his family. When Anne's diary was recovered after the war, her father arranged for it to be published. More than sixty million copies have been sold.

Below: Anne Frank, whose diary has touched the hearts of millions, in 1942. **Opposite:** Norman Rockwell's 1943 interpretation of Rosie the Riveter, icon of women who worked during World War II.

Rosie the Riveter
working woman (1941–1945)

*T*he May 29, 1943, cover of *The Saturday Evening Post* sports a Norman Rockwell painting of a woman in overalls, a work shirt, and goggles. Behind her is a flowing American flag. The muscles in her biceps and forearms are bulging; on her face is an expression of confidence and self-assuredness. She is on her lunch break, seated, her foot casually crushing a copy of *Mein Kampf*, her rivet gun resting in her lap along with her lunch box, which bears the name Rosie.

She is Rosie the Riveter, icon of women who flooded into the American workplace in unprecedented numbers during World War II. Rosie was celebrated in songs, movies, and posters as the woman who left hearth and home to pitch in and do her part for her country. The real Rosie wasn't any one woman but millions who became lumber and steel workers, electricians, welders, mechanics, scientists, police officers, and bus drivers to replace the millions of men who were mobilized for military service.

In 1940, as the United States prepared to enter World War II, President Roosevelt called for American industry to start producing war equipment. In 1941, the government started recruiting women to work factory assembly lines. Prior to this time, women (as well as men of color) had been subject to blatant discrimination, low pay, and job segregation. Now government and industry had no choice but to turn to these unwanted workers for the dangerous, heavy, or skilled labor for which women had previously been considered unqualified.

A massive propaganda campaign was launched to convince women and business leaders alike that women could—and had to—do the work. Posters showed competent, confident women working at imposing-looking equipment with captions like "Count on us! We won't let you down!" and "Women in the war—we can't win without them," and "The more women at work the sooner we will win!"

The total number of employed women increased from 12 million (27.4 percent of women in the United States) in 1940 to 18.2 million (35 percent) in 1944. Many women migrated from lower-paying jobs such as waitress, hairdresser, and teacher.

A lot of the women excelled at their jobs and found in them a new sense of mission and self-worth. "Never thought I could do such exacting work—and I'm real proud," said one assembly worker. Surveys done during the war showed that large numbers of Rosies wanted to keep their jobs after the war was over. Instead, they were subject to wholesale layoffs as industry made room for returning men. There was a huge backlash against the idea of employed women; by 1947, almost half of the 6 million women new to the workforce had left.

Rosie the Riveter changed women's and men's entrenched notions and expectations about what women are capable of doing. While the country then experienced a degree of amnesia, the women did not forget. Transformed by the experience, women came away with a new sense of self-worth, competence, financial independence, and pride at contributing to the war effort. One riveter said her wartime employment "was the first time in my life that I had the chance to prove that I could do something, and I did."

Above: Lucille Ball, beloved star of the television show *I Love Lucy*, with her husband and co-star, Desi Arnaz, and their onscreen son, Little Ricky. **Opposite:** Lucille Ball.

Lucille Ball
actor and producer (1911–1989)

The hilariously gifted Lucille Ball was perhaps the most well-known and beloved performer in the world—her popular television show *I Love Lucy* still airs in syndication in more than seventy-five countries and dozens of languages. With her superb timing, flawless physical comedy, and rubbery face, she created the memorable character of Lucy Ricardo, a wacky, scatterbrained wife who spent much of her time trying to break into show business at her perpetually exasperated husband's nightclub.

The woman who in 1996 topped *TV Guide*'s list of Fifty Greatest TV Stars of All Time was frequently told early in her career that she didn't have the talent to make it in show business. Growing up in Jamestown, New York, Ball started piano lessons at age five and, starstruck, quit high school at age fifteen to attend a drama school in New York City. Unable to make it on Broadway, she modeled, and she won bit parts and small roles in

movies over the next fifteen years, but stardom eluded her. "They always cast me wrong," Ball said, "but at least I always got work because I could scream, I could run, and I could certainly wear a mud pack."

On the set of the 1940 musical *Too Many Girls*, she met Cuban bandleader Desi Arnaz, and they married six months later. In 1950, she approached CBS with the concept for *I Love Lucy*, but network executives balked at the idea of the Latin Arnaz playing her husband. Finally, CBS reluctantly gave them a time slot, and they produced the show through their own production company, Desilu. Premiering on October 15, 1951, *I Love Lucy* was an overnight sensation. Averaging an amazing forty million viewers, the show never ranked below third in the weekly Nielsen ratings in the six years that it was on the air.

The show also made history behind the scenes. In the early days of television, shows were done live on New York sound stages and not recorded. Wishing to remain in Los Angeles, Ball and Arnaz decided to film their show before a live audience with a three-camera technique that allowed for later editing. They took a pay cut to absorb some of the technical costs but extracted one hundred percent of the rights for repeat airings—inventing the financially lucrative rerun. Desilu went on to produce more than eighteen shows, including *The Untouchables*, *Star Trek*, and *Mission Impossible*, and the television industry eventually relocated most of its production to the West Coast.

After divorcing Arnaz in 1960, Ball bought him out, becoming the first woman to head a major Hollywood television production company. "My ability comes from fairness and a knowledge of people," she said. "I ran my studio like I run my home, with understanding of people." It was said that she knew every person and every piece of equipment on the set by name. She sold Desilu in 1967 to Gulf & Western for $17 million. With her second husband, Gary Morton, she produced and starred in two more popular series: *The Lucy Show* and *Here's Lucy*.

The four-time Emmy winner credited her colleagues for her success. "I am not funny," Ball said. "My writers were funny. The situations were funny..... What I am is brave. I have never been scared. Not when I did movies, certainly not when I was a model, and not when I did *I Love Lucy*."

standing over a subway grate with the air blowing her skirt up. She was a bona fide star.

Monroe's 1954 marriage to Joe DiMaggio, the retired New York Yankees slugger, inspired enormous publicity but lasted only nine months. Monroe wanted to be taken seriously as an actor. She moved to New York and studied under Lee Strasberg at the Actors Studio. She started her own production company, Marilyn Monroe Productions, and sought out the company of intellectuals and artists. In 1956, she married playwright Arthur Miller.

Monroe did mature as an actor and received critical acclaim for her performances in *Bus Stop* (1956) and *Some Like it Hot* (1959), in which she showed greater depth and a talent for comedy. But she couldn't transcend her image. "That's the trouble—a sex symbol becomes a thing. I just hate to be a thing," she said. By this time, Monroe was suffering from depression. Hooked on prescription drugs, she made several suicide attempts. She died on August 5, 1962, from an overdose of sleeping pills.

Norma Jean Baker, the person, had ultimately become subsumed by Marilyn Monroe, the icon. Mocked during her lifetime for wishing to pursue an education, to improve her craft, and to be taken seriously, after her death, she is immortalized for the very misconceptions that drove her to despair. In her last interview before her death, she pleaded with the reporter, "Please don't make me a joke."

Below: Monroe dishes out a meal to grateful American soldiers in Korea.

Above: Clara "Mother" Hale celebrates her eighty-third birthday with some of the children being cared for at Hale House.

Clara McBride Hale
child care pioneer (1906–1993)

When Clara "Mother" Hale decided to retire at the age of sixty-four, she had raised forty foster children along with three of her own. "Then my daughter sent me a girl with an addict baby," she recalled. "Inside of two months I had twenty-two babies living in a five-room apartment." In 1969, Mother Hale opened the doors to Hale House, a Harlem brownstone in which she created a loving, safe environment for babies born drug-addicted or, later, with HIV/AIDS. Over the next twenty-five years, she nurtured more than one thousand babies and touched countless lives with her generous spirit and infinite love of children.

Clara grew up in Philadelphia in a home that was always filled with children, including her three siblings and lots of neighborhood kids. Orphaned at sixteen, she finished high school and began working as a domestic. She married Thomas Hale and they moved to Brooklyn to raise a family. Shortly after the birth of her third child, Hale was widowed. Rather than leave her kids to do domestic work, she decided to take in other people's children and became a licensed foster parent.

"I raised forty. Every one of them went to college, every one of them graduated, and they have lovely jobs," she said with great pride. "They're some of the nicest people. Anything they wanted to do, I backed them up. I have singers, dancers, preachers...schoolteachers, lawyers, doctors, anything else. No big name or anything, but they're happy."

Born with a host of problems, the addicted babies were then blessed with Hale's simple solution. "We hold them and rock them," she explained. "They love you to tell them how great they are, how good they are. Somehow, even at a young age, they understand that. They're happy and they turn out well." More heartbreaking was the fate of babies born with HIV, most of whom contracted AIDS. Hale made sure that her children's short lives were filled with loving attention and that they were made as comfortable as possible. "I want them to live a good life while they can and know someone loves them," she said. At a time when most people shunned anyone with AIDS, Hale set a courageous and compelling example.

Supported by private resources and government grants, Hale House is now run by Clara Hale's daughter, Lorraine Hale, who earned a Ph.D. in child development. Called an American hero by President Ronald Reagan in 1985, Clara Hale shrugged off the accolade. "I'm not an American hero," she said simply. "I'm a person that loves children."

LASTING LEGACY

Gloria Steinem
activist and writer (1934–)

At the end of many of her speeches, Gloria Steinem urges each member of the audience to "commit an outrageous act in the cause of simple justice" within twenty-four hours and promises that she will, too. Like the proverbial pebble in the lake, she has stirred millions of people to action and improved countless women's lives in her almost thirty years as a feminist writer and organizer.

Much of the progress in the status of women during the second wave of American feminism has been inspired by her leadership, vision, and compassion. She also advocates for lesbians and gay men, people of color, poor people, and the disenfranchised. In her inspiring speeches, best-selling books, and insightful articles, Steinem laces her razor-sharp analysis of gender issues and other oppressions with an abundance of humor and grace, often winning over resistant critics.

Her mother, suffering from anxiety and sometimes delusions, was rarely able to take care of young Gloria; after her parents divorced, she in fact took care of her mother. Having planned to tap-dance her way out of her hometown of Toledo, Ohio, Steinem instead got into Smith College and graduated with a degree in government in 1956. On her way to India to study on a fellowship, Steinem discovered she was pregnant and, frightened and alone, had a legal abortion in England.

Two years later, Steinem returned to the United States to work as a freelance journalist. Deeply influenced by Gandhian activism, she also joined causes radical for the day, like student organizing, the civil rights movement, and the United Farm Workers crusade for migrant workers' rights.

In 1969, Steinem reported on a speakout in New York City in which women testified to the dangers they withstood in obtaining illegal abortions. She was profoundly affected. "If one in three or four adult women shares this experience," she later wrote, "why should each of us be made to feel criminal and alone? How much power would we ever have if we had no power over the fate of our own bodies?" Steinem read all the feminist literature she could find and, despite her tremendous fear of public speaking, traveled around the country promoting this new movement.

Two years later, she co-founded *Ms.*—the first national women's magazine created and controlled by women. Its premiere issue sold out, and *Ms.* became known as the magazine of record for the feminist movement. To this day, as Steinem travels, women tell her how the magazine touched, changed, or practically saved their lives.

Steinem was also a founder of the National Women's Political Caucus, the Ms. Foundation for Women, the Coalition of Labor Union Women, and Voters for Choice.

In 1992, she wrote *Revolution from Within: A Book of Self-Esteem*, an exploration of the relationship between personal wholeness and social change. "Self-esteem isn't everything," she

Below: Influential feminist activist and writer Gloria Steinem in 1966.

Above: Steinem relishes the time she grabs at *Ms.* magazine, in between an exhausting schedule of speaking events, rallies, fundraisers, and book tours.

wrote, "it's just that there's nothing without it." An embracing, hopeful work that drew on her own experiences, *Revolution from Within* was a number-one bestseller and has been translated into fifteen languages.

"Women may be the one group that grows more radical with age," Steinem wrote in *Outrageous Acts and Everyday Rebellions*, her popular collection of essays first published in 1983. Now in her sixties, Steinem, who patiently and endlessly tried to answer the question, "What do women want?" without coming across as an "angry feminist," no longer holds back. "But it's a healthy anger," she writes, "that warms my heart, loosens my tongue, leaves me feeling ever more important and energized, and gives me a what-the-hell kind of courage."

Gladys Tantaquidgeon
anthropologist and medicine woman (1899–)

As a child growing up on land in Connecticut that was once the Mohegan reservation, Gladys Tantaquidgeon learned the ways and stories of her people from the elder women of her tribe. She learned which foods are to be hunted and gathered during which seasons. She learned herbal healing methods. She learned the Mohegan value of living in harmony with all kinds of neighbors. She learned about the Makiawisug, the invisible little people of the woodlands to whom traditional Mohegans make offerings. And she remembered it all. Decades later, Tantaquidgeon's memory and her passion for preserving Mohegan culture were her tribe's salvation.

In 1919, encouraged by anthropologist Frank G. Speck, who had visited her family home while doing research on the

Mohegans, Tantaquidgeon began eight years of study in anthropology under his tutelage at the University of Pennsylvania. In the 1930s, she did social work on reservations in the western United States and then worked for the federal government's Indian Arts and Crafts Board.

In the meantime, her family had started a Mohegan museum in a small stone building behind their home in Montville, Connecticut. In 1947, Tantaquidgeon returned home to run the museum with her brother, who had become the Mohegan chief. "My family has the responsibility to care for and protect the legacy of the Mohegans," she said, "to inform all who come here about our people, about the rich Mohegan culture and traditions."

The Mohegan people had been living in what is now southeastern Connecticut for decades before the arrival of Europeans. But as the newcomers pursued their campaign of taking Indian land, converting everyone to Christianity, and banning Native American languages, the distinct culture of the Mohegans, like those of many tribes, started to erode. The official policy of the U.S. government up until the 1960s was to destroy distinctive tribal identity and to force Indians to assimilate to white culture and laws.

In the late 1970s, as a result of decades of agitation by Native Americans, the U.S. government started to concede a certain degree of autonomy for tribes that could prove they had existed continuously "from historical times to the present." At stake were major land claims, millions of dollars in federal grants, a degree of self-determination, and simple justice.

Mohegan researchers presented to the Bureau of Indian Affairs stacks of documentation of their history as a distinct people. The government rejected their claim, citing lack of evidence of continuing traditional tribal activities in the second half of the twentieth century. Tantaquidgeon then produced hundreds of documents—meticulously maintained birth, death, and marriage records; correspondence; and accounts of cultural activities—which she had stored in Tupperware containers under her bed. It was her testimony and the records she had collected over many years that finally persuaded the federal government to recognize the approximately one thousand remaining Mohegans as a Native tribe.

As for Tantaquidgeon, she still maintains the Mohegan museum, presiding over its hand-woven baskets, bowls, jewelry, tools, dolls, and beaded ceremonial costumes. "Most people who come here are amazed that Mohegans are still alive," she said. "All their lives they've heard the old saying about the last of the Mohegans."

Below: Gladys Tantaquidgeon and her brother, Harold, on the grounds of the Mohegan museum they built with their father in 1931 to preserve their heritage.

Diana, Princess of Wales
humanitarian (1961–1997)

The whole world watched her transformation from a shy romantic to an affectionate mother, to a lonely public figure, to a compassionate humanitarian, to a savvy divorcée. The sudden death of Diana, Princess of Wales, at the age of thirty-six stunned the world, inspiring an unprecedented outpouring of love and grief and a reassessment of her life.

Lady Diana Spencer was born into an aristocratic family. Her father was the Eighth Earl Spencer, and she grew up with her three siblings on the family estate, Althorp, just a stone's throw from the royal family's Sandringham retreat. When this private-kindergarten teacher's aide married Charles, Prince of Wales, heir to the throne of England, on July 29, 1981, three-quarters of a billion television viewers around the world watched "the Marriage of the Century."

The marriage proved to be famously disastrous. They had little in common: he was traditional, erudite, interested in architecture, gardening, and horses. Diana had a wicked sense of humor and loved pop music, dancing, and being with her children, William and Harry, whom she tried to expose to a world outside of palace life. Diana and Charles's separation in 1992 was messy, very public, and often embarrassing. When they divorced four years later, she was stripped of the title Her Royal Highness, but she remained Princess of Wales, was allowed to continue to live at Kensington Palace, and shared custody of the children.

Throughout her public life, Diana visited hospitals, hospices, and battered women's shelters. She raised money and awareness for causes such as AIDS, cancer, leprosy, and homelessness. In the months before her death, she drew public attention to the movement for a global ban on land mines, which kill or maim twenty-six thousand people each year. "I am not a political figure," she said. "I am a humanitarian figure, and I always will be."

In a televised 1995 interview, Diana said she wanted to become the "queen of people's hearts"—and although she was every inch the aristocrat, ordinary people felt that she had a "common touch." Perhaps because her personal dramas had been played out on such a public stage, they felt that they could relate to this insecure, flawed, complicated woman.

The unblinking eye of the media was a blessing and a curse. When Diana wanted to have her side of the story told, she would confide in sympathetic reporters. The photographers who followed her everywhere took pictures of her hugging people with AIDS and comforting land-mine victims in Angola and Bosnia. But the "most photographed woman in the world" was hounded merciless-

Below: Princess Diana holds a shy, young Prince Harry in Spain where they were vacationing in 1986. **Opposite:** Diana greets local people in the mountain village of Banauti, Nepal, 1993.

ly by aggressive, intrusive paparazzi who sold intimate scenes to tabloids for big money.

Toward the end of her life, Diana seemed to have turned a corner. Friends observed that she seemed more settled and self-confident; she had just returned from a vacation on the Mediterranean with her new lover, Dodi Fayed. On August 30, 1997, after leaving the Ritz Hotel in Paris, the car carrying Diana, Fayed, their driver, and their bodyguard was pursued by a pack of photographers and crashed at a speed of 120 miles (192 km) per hour; only the bodyguard survived.

For days, thousands of people descended on Kensington Palace, leaving bouquets of flowers that spread out, six or seven deep, for hundreds of yards. Around the world, people gathered in public meeting places to watch her funeral, held at Westminster Abbey; perhaps as many as two billion watched on television.

A trust, established in the princess' name to support her causes, was flooded with donations of more than $200 million in the first weekend alone, ensuring that her legacy will reflect what she truly cared about, not what others made her out to be.

Selected Bibliography

Ashby, Ruth, and Ohrn, Deborah Gore, eds. *Herstory: Women Who Changed the World*. New York: Viking, 1995.

Badran, Margot, and Cooke, Miriam, eds. *Opening the Gates: A Century of Arab Feminist Writing*. Bloomington, IN: Indiana University Press, 1990.

Barker-Benfield, G.J., and Catherine Clinton, eds. *Portraits of American Women: From Settlement to the Present*. New York: St. Martin's Press, 1991.

Bertsch, Sharon McGrayne. *Nobel Prize Women in Science: Their Lives, Struggles and Momentous Discoveries*. New York: Carol Publishing Group, 1992.

Colman, Penny. *Rosie the Riveter: Women Working on the Home Front in World War II*. New York: Crown, 1995.

Davidson, Sue. *A Heart in Politics: Jeannette Rankin and Patsy T. Mink*. Seattle, WA: Seal Press, 1994.

De Beauvoir, Simone, *The Second Sex*. New York: Bantam, 1952.

Delamotte, Eugenia; Meeker, Natania; and O'Barr, Jean, eds. *Women Imagine Change: A Global Anthology of Women's Resistance from 600 B.C.E. to Present* New York: Routledge, 1997.

Ferraro, Geraldine A., with Linda Bird Francke. *Ferraro: My Story*. New York: Bantam Books, 1985.

Frank, Anne. *Anne Frank: The Diary of a Young Girl*. Mooyaart, B.M., trans. New York: Doubleday, 1967.

Friedan, Betty. *The Feminine Mystique*. New York: W.W. Norton, 1963.

Giddings, Paula. *When and Where I Enter: The Impact of Black Women on Race and Sex in America*. New York: Bantam Books, 1984.

Hine, Darlene Clark, ed. *Black Women in America: An Historical Encyclopedia, Volumes I and II*. Brooklyn, NY: Carlson Publishing, 1993.

Kass-Simon, G., and Farnes, Patricia. *Women of Science: Righting the Record*. Bloomington, IN: Indiana University Press, 1990.

Lanker, Brian. *I Dream a World: Portraits of Black Women Who Changed America*. New York: Stewart, Tabori & Chang, 1989.

Maggio, Rosalie, ed. *The New Beacon Book of Quotations by Women*. Boston: Beacon Press, 1996.

Mankiller, Wilma, and Wallace, Michael. *Mankiller: A Chief and Her People*. New York: St. Martin's Press, 1993.

McHenry, Robert, ed. *Her Heritage: A Biographical Encyclopedia of Famous American Women* (CD-ROM). Cambridge, MA: Pilgrim New Media, 1994.

Menchu, Rigoberta. *I, Rigoberta Menchu: An Indian Woman in Guatemala*. Elisabeth Burgos- Debray, ed. Ann Wright, trans. London: Verso, 1986.

Rose, Phyllis. *The Norton Book of Women's Lives*. New York: W.W. Norton, 1993.

Sartori, Eva Martin, and Zimmerman, Dorothy Wynne, eds. *French Women Writers*. Lincoln, NE: University of Nebraska Press, 1991.

Showalter, Elaine; Baechler, Lea; and Litz, A. Walton, eds. *Modern American Women Writers: Profiles of Their Lives and Works—From the 1870s to the Present*. New York: Collier Books, 1993.

Sicherman, Barbara, and Green, Carol Hurd, eds. *Notable American Women, The Modern Period: A Biographical Dictionary*. Cambridge, MA: The Bell Knap Press of Harvard University Press, 1980.

Smith, Valerie; Baechler, Lea; and Litz, A. Walton, eds. *African American Writers: Profiles of Their Lives and Works—From the 1700s to the Present*. New York: Collier Books, 1993.

Steinem, Gloria. *Marilyn*. New York: Plume, 1987.

Steinem, Gloria. *Moving Beyond Words*. New York: Simon & Schuster, 1994

Steinem, Gloria. *Outrageous Acts and Everyday Rebellions*. New York: Holt, Rinehart and Winston, 1983.

Telgen, Diane, and Kamp, Jim eds. *Notable Hispanic American Women*. Detroit: Gale Research, 1993.

Vernon, Lillian. *An Eye for Winners: How I Built One of America's Greatest Direct-Mail Businesses*. New York: HarperCollins, 1996.

Walker, Alice. *The Color Purple*. New York: Washington Square Press, 1982.

Whitfield, Eileen. *Pickford: The Woman Who Made Hollywood*. Lexington, KY: The University Press of Kentucky, 1997.

BIBLIOGRAPHY

173

175

Photo Credits

The publishers have made every effort to trace the copyright owners of the illustrations in this book, but the nature of the material has meant that this has not always been possible. Any person or organization we have failed to reach, despite our efforts, is invited to contact the Photo Director.

Corbis-Bettmann photography*:
*All images are credited "UPI/Corbis Bettmann" unless listed below)

Agence France Presse/Corbis-Bettmann: pp. 53 middle left, 68, 69, 71 top right, 76, 77; **Corbis-Bettmann:** pp. 7 top, 13 top center, 14, 18, 31 middle center, 33, 34, 41, 71 middle center, 74, 75, 89 top right, 89 middle center and right, 89 bottom right, 94 top, 96, 97, 100, 104, 105, 112, 131 top right, 132, 133, 151 middle right, 155, 156 top, front endpaper: Curie, Anderson; back endpaper: Kahlo, Addams, McLeod-Bethune, M. Graham; **Frank Driggs/Corbis-Bettmann:** pp. 89 top center, 101, front endpaper: Holiday; **Peter C. Jones/Alex Gotfryd/ Corbis-Bettmann:** pp. 131 bottom center, 142, back endpaper: Walters; **Penguin/Corbis-Bettmann:** pp. 151 bottom center, 162, 164; **Florence and Carol Reiff/Corbis-Bettmann:** p. 102; **Reuters/Corbis-Bettmann:** pp. 11 bottom right, 22, 25, 29 top, 108, 109, 111 bottom center and right, 118, 122, 129, 131 top center, 144, 145, 170, 171, front endpaper: Thatcher; back endpaper: Hill/Streisand, Diana, Angelou; **Springer/Corbis-Bettmann:** pp. 7 bottom, 11 bottom left, 151 top left, 151 middle center, 160, 163, front endpaper: Frank; **Underwood & Underwood/Corbis-Bettmann:** pp. 2, 35, 116, 151 top right, 158

All other photography:

AP / Wide World Photos: pp. 51, 59, 71 bottom left, 83, 98, 128, 146

Archive Photos: pp. 17, 43 top, back endpaper (O'Keeffe); ©Fred H. Conrad/NYT Co.: p. 45, ©Reuters/Wang Yin Chang: p. 53 middle right, 66, front endpaper (Ling); ©Reuters/Christine Grunnet: p. 67; ©Bernard Gotfryd: pp. 151 top center, 167

Art Resource: p. 99

Courtesy of Ann Bancroft: p. 50; ©Per Breiehagen: p. 31 bottom left

©1998 Marianne Barcellona: p. 168

Special Collections, University Archives, California Polytechnic State University: pp. 31 middle left, 37 bottom

Courtesy of the Children's Television Workshop: ©Philip Greenberg: p. 86

Courtesy of the Creative Arts Book Co.: pp. 119 (Photo by Deborah Storms), 120

Courtesy of the Gladys Tantaquidgeon Museum: p. 169

Globe Photos: ©Adam Scull: p. 27; ©Judie Burstein: p. 131 bottom left; ©Fitzroy Barrett: p. 149

©Hearst San Simeon State Historical Monument: p. 37 top

Kobal Collection: pp. 21, 29 bottom

Courtesy of Nell Merlino / SCA: ©Brooke Williams: pp. 71 top left, 87

Courtesy of the Museum of Modern Art: p. 103

Photo Courtesy of the Norman Rockwell Museum at Stockbridge: p. 161

©Joy E. Scheller: p. 143

Photographs and Prints Division, Schomburg Center for Research in Black Culture, The New York Public Library, Astor, Lenox and Tilden Foundations: pp. 71 top center, 72, 73, 125

Courtesy of Eka Esu-Williams: pp. 111 bottom left, 126